EDITOR: Maryanne Blacker

FOOD EDITOR: Pamela Clark

• • •

ASSISTANT FOOD EDITOR: Barbara Northwood

HOME ECONOMISTS: Jon Allen, Wendy Berecry,
Jan Castorina, Jane Cleary, Karen Green, Sue Hipwell,
Louise Sakiris, Kathy Wharton

EDITORIAL COORDINATOR: Elizabeth Hooper

KITCHEN ASSISTANT: Amy Wong

• • •

STYLISTS: Jacqui Hing, Carolyn Fienberg

COVER STYLIST: Jane Hann

COVER PHOTOGRAPHER: Robert Taylor

• • •

HOME LIBRARY STAFF:

ASSISTANT EDITOR: Beverley Hudec

ART DIRECTOR: Paula Wooller

DESIGNER: Robbylee Phelan

EDITORIAL COORDINATOR: Fiona Nicholas

• • •

ACP PUBLISHER: Richard Walsh

ACP DEPUTY PUBLISHER: Nick Chan

• • •

Produced by The Australian Women's Weekly Home Library.
Typeset by ACP Colour Graphics Pty Ltd, Sydney. Printed by
Dai Nippon Co., Ltd in Japan.
Published by ACP Publishing, 54 Park Street Sydney.
♦ AUSTRALIA: Distributed by Network Distribution Company,
54 Park Street Sydney, (02) 282 8777.
♦ UNITED KINGDOM: Distributed in the U.K. by Australian
Consolidated Press (UK) Ltd, 20 Galowhill Rd, Brackmills,
Northampton NN4 OEE (0604) 760 456.
♦ CANADA: Distributed in Canada by Whitecap
Books Ltd, 1086 West 3rd St,
North Vancouver V7P 3J6 (604) 980 9852.
♦ NEW ZEALAND: Distributed in New Zealand by Netlink
Distribution Company, 17B Hargreaves St, Level 5,
College Hill, Auckland 1 (9) 302 7616.
♦ SOUTH AFRICA: Distributed in South Africa by Intermag,
PO Box 57394, Springfield 2137 (011) 493 3200.

• • •

Celebration Cookbook

Includes index.
ISBN 0 949128 05 8.

1. Cookery. 2. Holiday Cookery.
3. Christmas Cookery. (Series: Australian
Women's Weekly Home Library).

641.5'68

• • •

• • •

COVER: Roast Turkey with Apricot and Water
Chestnut Seasoning, page 5.
*China, champagne glasses from Villeroy & Boch. Ribbon,
gold chest, tassels, serviette, serviette rings from Between
the Sheets. Cutlery from David Jones Pty Ltd.*
OPPOSITE: Clockwise from top: Duck Terrine, page 26,
Traditional Christmas Glazed Leg of Ham, page 13,
Loin of Pork with Orange Seasoning, page 4,
Seafood Platter, page 26, Australian Christmas Cake, page 16,
Fruit Mince Tarts, page 51.
*Tablecloth, cutlery, bucket, wine and champagne glasses from
Studio Haus; china 'Manoir' by Villeroy & Boch; salad bowl from
Kosta Boda; Christmas tree and decorations from Mei and Picchi.*
BACK COVER: Sweet Heart, page 125.

CELEBRATION COOKBOOK

We have compiled a book simply brimming with
wonderful recipes and information to help you make your
celebratory events a great success. Favourite Christmas cakes
and puddings with rich sauces and icings, baked ham with
delicious glazes, turkey with tasty seasonings and hints on how
to carve both meats are included. There is a terrific
selection of home-made gifts, party food and cakes for children,
delectable suggestions for Easter celebrations and a host of
dinner parties to suit any special occasion including birthdays,
anniversaries, New Year or even a christening.

Pamela Clark

FOOD EDITOR

BRITISH & NORTH AMERICAN READERS: Please note that Australian
cup and spoon measurements are metric. A quick conversion guide
appears on page 128.
A glossary explaining unfamiliar terms and ingredients is on page 126.

Clockwise from front: Loin of Pork with Orange Seasoning; Roast Turkey with Rosemary and Bacon Seasoning; Goose with Apple and Chestnut Seasoning

Hearty Fare For A
MERRY CHRISTMAS

A Christmas gathering inevitably signals lots of hard work in the kitchen. To ease the burden we have included valuable advice on glazing, seasoning, carving, cooking and decorating the food.

GOOSE WITH APPLE AND CHESTNUT SEASONING

This recipe is not suitable to freeze or microwave.

3kg goose
60g butter, melted
CHESTNUT SEASONING
2 bacon rashers, chopped
1 stick celery, chopped
1 onion, chopped
440g can pie apple
½ x 440g can unsweetened chestnut puree
3 cups stale breadcrumbs
1 teaspoon dried thyme leaves
SHERRY SAUCE
1 tablespoon plain flour
1½ cups water
1 chicken stock cube, crumbled
2 tablespoons dry sherry

Remove neck and giblets from cavity, rinse goose well and pat dry. Spoon seasoning into cavity until three-quarters full (seasoning will expand a little during cooking). Secure neck flap under goose with skewer, secure wings to body with skewers, sew up cavity with needle and cotton, tie legs together firmly. Place goose on wire rack over baking dish, brush goose with butter, bake in moderate oven (allowing about 30 minutes per 500g), brush goose with butter or pan drippings during the cooking time. Serve hot with sauce.

Chestnut Seasoning: Combine bacon, celery and onion in saucepan, cook, stirring, until onion is soft, transfer to bowl. Stir in apple and chestnut then breadcrumbs and thyme.

Sherry Sauce: Discard pan drippings except for about 1 tablespoon. Blend flour into baking dish, stir constantly over heat until lightly browned, gradually add water and stock cube, stir until sauce boils and thickens, stir in sherry.

LOIN OF PORK WITH ORANGE SEASONING

Ask the butcher to bone out a loin of pork for you, and to leave a long flap. This recipe is not suitable to freeze or microwave.

1 loin of pork (12 chops)
oil
salt
SEASONING
2 cups stale breadcrumbs
2 tablespoons grated orange rind
2 tablespoons chopped fresh chives
30g butter, melted
1 egg
SAUCE
1 tablespoon plain flour
1½ cups water
1 chicken stock cube, crumbled
1 tablespoon brandy
¼ cup orange juice

Place seasoning along centre of flap of pork, roll firmly, tie securely with string at 2cm intervals. Place loin on rack over baking dish, brush with oil, rub with a little salt. Bake in moderate oven for about 2 hours or until pork is tender; remove string from pork.

If serving pork hot, serve with sauce, or if serving cold, allow pork to come to room temperature, then refrigerate several hours, or overnight before slicing.

Seasoning: Combine all ingredients in bowl, mix well.

Sauce: Drain fat from baking dish, leave about 1 tablespoon fat in dish. Add flour to dish, stir constantly over heat until mixture is lightly browned. Gradually stir in water and stock cube, stir constantly over heat until sauce boils and thickens; stir in brandy and orange juice, reheat the sauce just before serving.

ROAST TURKEY WITH HAZELNUT BUTTER

Turkey can be prepared by pushing the butter under the skin up to 1 day ahead or freezing for up to 2 months. Season after turkey is thawed. This recipe is not suitable to microwave.

4kg turkey
½ cup water
oil
HAZELNUT BUTTER
185g soft butter
2 cloves garlic, crushed
¼ cup whole roasted hazelnuts, finely chopped
2 tablespoons chopped parsley
SAUCE
1 litre (4 cups) water
1 bay leaf
few whole black peppercorns
1 onion, sliced
¼ cup plain flour
¼ cup dry sherry
½ cup cranberry sauce

Remove neck and giblets from inside turkey and reserve for making the sauce. Rinse turkey under cold water, pat dry inside and out. Tuck wings under body. Loosen skin over breast and tops of legs using fingers or the handle of the wooden spoon, as shown.

Hazelnut Butter: Beat butter in bowl with wooden spoon until smooth. Stir in garlic, hazelnuts and parsley, push butter under skin of turkey. Be careful not to break skin of turkey.

Fill cavity of turkey loosely with seasoning of your choice (seasoning will swell during cooking). Sew opening of turkey by sewing it with needle and coloured cotton (this makes it easier to see to remove).

Place a wire rack in a baking dish, add water to the dish, place turkey on rack; tuck trimmed neck flap under the body; tie legs securely together. Brush turkey evenly all over with oil.

Bake in moderate oven for about 2½ hours or until turkey is tender, basting about every 20 minutes with pan juices. You will need to cover breast and legs of turkey with foil after 1 hour of cooking so that skin does not darken too much.

While turkey is cooking, begin to prepare the sauce. Combine neck and giblets in saucepan with water, bay leaf, peppercorns and onion. Bring to the boil, reduce heat, simmer, covered, 1 hour; strain, reserve stock for sauce.

Remove turkey from dish, place on oven tray, cover with foil, keep warm while completing sauce.

Sauce: Drain fat from dish, leaving about 2 tablespoons fat in dish. Add flour to dish, stir constantly over heat until mixture starts to brown. Gradually stir in 2½ cups reserved stock, sherry and cranberry sauce. Stir until sauce boils and thickens, strain, serve hot over turkey.

SEASONINGS

Mix and match these seasonings to suit your own taste. The flavours will complement turkey, duck, goose, chicken or pork. Some are based on rice, others on breadcrumbs. When making breadcrumbs, leave bread exposed to the air for several hours to dry out a little, then blend or process to give fine crumbs. Stale bread can be grated, but this is time consuming.

We used white bread with crusts removed, for most of these recipes, but use wholemeal bread if you prefer. Excess breadcrumbs will freeze perfectly for several months. The seasoning in

Roast Turkey with Hazelnut Butter

turkeys and chickens tends to become soggy if frozen inside the birds.

The quantities given for all the seasonings are sufficient for average-sized turkeys (about 3kg); reduce the quantities as necessary for chickens and the like. Seasonings do not freeze well as a general rule, results are much better if seasoning is made freshly.

Remember not to over-fill the cavities in the birds as seasoning will swell during the cooking; three-quarters fill the cavity for best results.

Rice-based seasonings work best if the rice is very slightly undercooked.

ROSEMARY AND BACON SEASONING

5 bacon rashers, chopped
2 onions, chopped
1 teaspoon dried rosemary leaves
2 sticks celery, chopped
125g mushrooms, sliced
4 cups stale breadcrumbs
Cook bacon in frying pan until crisp, remove from pan. Add onions to pan, cook until onions are soft. Add rosemary, celery and mushrooms, cook for 1 minute, remove from heat, stir in breadcrumbs and bacon.

APRICOT AND WATER CHESTNUT SEASONING

You will need to cook 1⅓ cups rice for this recipe.

60g butter
1 onion, chopped
2 cloves garlic, crushed
6 green shallots, chopped
1 teaspoon paprika
4 cups cooked long-grain rice
280g can water chestnuts, drained, chopped
2 sticks celery, chopped
⅓ cup chopped dried apricots
½ cup stale breadcrumbs
1 egg, lightly beaten
2 tablespoons chopped parsley
Melt butter in saucepan, add onion and garlic, cook until onion is soft. Add shallots and paprika, cook 1 minute. Combine rice, water chestnuts, onion mixture, celery, apricots, breadcrumbs, egg and parsley in bowl and mix well.

SPINACH AND PINE NUT SEASONING

1 tablespoon pine nuts
3 bacon rashers, chopped
1 clove garlic, crushed
1 onion, chopped
1½ cups short grain rice
1 chicken stock cube, crumbled
2 cups water
250g packet frozen chopped spinach
Place pine nuts in large frying pan, stir over heat until lightly browned, remove from pan immediately. Add bacon to pan, cook until crisp, add garlic and onion, cook until onion is soft. Stir in rice, stock cube, water and unthawed spinach. Bring to the boil, reduce heat, simmer uncovered 15 minutes, stirring occasionally. Stir in pine nuts.

RICE AND NUT SEASONING

You will need to cook 1 cup rice for this recipe.

3 cups cooked long-grain rice
250g sausage mince
1 small onion, chopped
1 stick celery, chopped
60g (½ cup) chopped pecans or walnuts
1 clove garlic, crushed
1 egg, lightly beaten
2 teaspoons mixed herbs
Combine all ingredients in large bowl, mix well.

APPLE AND APRICOT SEASONING

⅓ cup chopped dried apricots
30g butter
1 onion, chopped
2 sticks celery, chopped
1 apple, chopped
1 tablespoon dry sherry
500g sausage mince
2 cups stale breadcrumbs
¼ cup chopped parsley
1 teaspoon dried thyme leaves

Place apricots in saucepan, cover with water, bring to the boil, reduce heat, simmer covered 5 minutes or until just tender, drain. Place in large bowl. Melt butter in frying pan, add onion, celery and apple, cook 2 minutes stirring. Add to apricots, stir in sherry.

Add mince to pan, cook, stirring, until mince changes colour, drain, add to apricot mixture with remaining ingredients; mix well.

WHOLEMEAL BACON SEASONING

2 bacon rashers, chopped
15g butter
1 onion, chopped
1 carrot, chopped
250g baby mushrooms, quartered
1 tablespoon brandy
1 teaspoon ground sage
2 teaspoons Worcestershire sauce
60g butter, extra
1 clove garlic, crushed
8 slices wholemeal bread
¼ cup chopped parsley

Cook bacon in frying pan until soft, add butter, onion and carrot, cook, stirring, for 5 minutes. Add mushrooms, cook few minutes or until mushrooms are just soft. Add brandy, sage and sauce, cook, stirring, for 2 minutes.

Melt extra butter in separate pan, add garlic. Remove crusts from bread, discard crusts. Cut bread into small cubes, place cubes in single layer on oven tray, drizzle evenly with garlic butter. Bake in moderate oven for about 30 minutes or until bread is crisp. Add bread to vegetable mixture with parsley.

CURRIED RICE AND APRICOT SEASONING

You will need to cook 1 cup rice for this recipe.

⅓ cup chopped dried apricots
4 bacon rashers, chopped
1 onion, chopped
2 teaspoons curry powder
2½ cups cooked long-grain rice
1 cup stale breadcrumbs

Cook apricots in boiling water for 5 minutes until slightly softened, drain.

HOW TO CARVE A TURKEY

There is no need to worry when carving a large turkey. Our step by step pictures make the task simple and show how to get the most from the turkey.

1 Cut off wing, then cut off the hindquarter on the same side, cutting through the thigh bone at top joint where it joins the body.

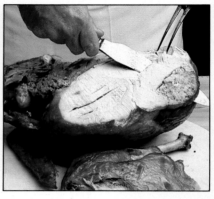

3 Carve across the breast at top so these slices incorporate some of the seasoning.

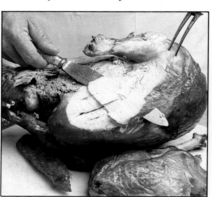

2 Turn bird on its side; place cut-off wing and hindquarter under bird to help keep it firm. Start carving breast up towards neck end. Take care when holding the blade towards you.

4 Carve leg and wing and incorporate this meat with breast meat. Turn bird over and carve the second side in the same way.

Cook bacon, onion and curry powder in frying pan until onion is soft, remove from heat. Stir in rice, breadcrumbs and apricots.

LOIN OF LAMB WITH MINT GLAZE

You will need to cook ⅓ cup of rice for this recipe. Ask butcher to make sure there is a long flap on loin as this will hold the seasoning securely. Have butcher bone out loin to make carving easier. This recipe is not suitable to freeze or microwave.

30g butter
1 small onion, chopped

1 stick celery, finely chopped
1 teaspoon dried tarragon leaves
1 tablespoon chopped fresh mint
1 cup cooked rice
¼ cup whole roasted hazelnuts, chopped
1 egg yolk
1 loin lamb (about 8 chops)
MINT GLAZE
2 tablespoons water
⅓ cup brown vinegar
2 teaspoons gelatine
1 tablespoon sugar
¼ cup chopped fresh mint

Melt butter in saucepan, add onion and celery, cook until onion is soft. Add tarragon, mint and rice, cook, stirring, for

Loin of Lamb with Mint Glaze

ABOVE: Chicken Galantine. RIGHT: Duck with Cranberry Sauce

few minutes. Remove from heat, stir in hazelnuts and egg yolk.

Spread loin of lamb out flat, place rice mixture on flap, roll up fairly tightly, secure loin with string. Stand on rack over baking dish, brush loin with a little oil. Bake in moderate oven for about 1½ hours or until lamb is tender. Cool to room temperature, then refrigerate for several hours before brushing several times with mint glaze.

Mint Glaze: Combine water and vinegar in saucepan, add gelatine and sugar. Bring to the boil, stirring constantly, add mint. Cool to room temperature before glazing lamb. Mixture should be about the consistency of unbeaten egg white.

CHICKEN GALANTINE

Galantine can be made 2 days ahead if desired. This recipe is not suitable to freeze or microwave.

No. 15 chicken
1 carrot, chopped
1 onion, chopped
1 stick celery, chopped
¼ teaspoon dried thyme leaves
4 whole black peppercorns
2 litres (8 cups) cold water
PORK AND VEAL SEASONING
1 tablespoon pistachio nuts
125g chicken livers
30g butter
1 onion
375g pork and veal mince

2 bacon rashers, finely chopped
2 tablespoons drained canned green peppercorns
1 egg
Bone chicken using small, sharp knife or scalpel. Cut off wing tips at second joint. Then cut through skin of chicken, down centre back. Separate flesh from backbone on one side with tip of knife. Then, following shape of bones of chicken, gradually ease flesh away from bones. Repeat the process with the other side of the chicken.

Holding the rib cage away from the chicken, gently cut breastbone from flesh.

Hold up the thigh with one hand, cut around the top of bone to remove

Table: Swatow Imports; platter: Wedgwood

flesh, scrape down the bone to next joint, cut around flesh again, scrape down to the end. Pull bone out and cut away. Repeat process with other leg bone and with both wings. Turn flesh of legs and wings inside chicken.

Spoon half the prepared seasoning down centre of chicken and arrange chicken livers in single row down centre of seasoning. Cover with the remaining seasoning, then fold one side of chicken over the other side. Place chicken on one end of the cheesecloth and roll up. Tie each end with string, then tie at 5cm intervals to keep a good shape while cooking.

Place chicken bones and carcass in large saucepan, add carrot, onion, cel-ery, thyme, peppercorns and water. Bring to the boil, reduce heat, simmer covered 1½ hours. Strain liquid and return to saucepan. Discard bones and vegetables. You should have at least 6 cups of liquid, if not, add water to make up to 6 cups.

Place chicken in saucepan, bring to the boil, cover, reduce heat, simmer covered 1½ hours. Allow chicken to cool in stock, refrigerate overnight.

Remove chicken from stock and unwrap the chicken.

Pour jellied stock into saucepan, heat until melted. Pour through fine strainer into bowl, refrigerate until nearly set.

Using a pastry brush, brush aspic over chicken (a decorative garnish of celery leaves or shallots can be put on top of chicken first). Or cut chicken into slices, arrange slightly overlapping slices on large serving plate, brush aspic over each slice. Refrigerate until set.

Pork and Veal Seasoning: Place pistachio nuts in bowl, cover with boiling water, stand 10 minutes. Peel away shells and brown skin, cut nuts in half. Clean and trim livers.

Melt butter in frying pan, add onion, cook until onion is soft. Remove from heat and place in bowl, with mince, bacon, peppercorns, egg and nuts, mix all ingredients well.

Serves 6 to 8.

9

DUCK WITH CRANBERRY SAUCE

This recipe is not suitable to freeze or microwave.

30g butter
2 tablespoons oil
No. 18 duck
¼ cup orange juice
2 tablespoons sugar
1½ tablespoons brown vinegar
1 chicken stock cube, crumbled
2 cups water
¼ cup cranberry sauce
2 teaspoons cornflour
2 teaspoons water, extra
2 tablespoons dry vermouth

Heat butter and oil in baking dish, brush duck with butter mixture. Put a wire rack in baking dish, place duck on top. Bake in moderate oven for about 1½ hours or until duck is tender, basting frequently with pan juices.

Combine orange juice, sugar, vinegar, stock cube, water and cranberry sauce in saucepan, bring to the boil, boil rapidly until reduced by half. Remove duck from baking dish and keep warm. Pour off all the fat from the baking dish, place dish on top of stove. Add sauce to dish, bring to the boil, strain sauce into saucepan, stir in blended cornflour and extra water, stir constantly over heat until sauce boils and thickens. Remove from heat, stir in vermouth.

PINEAPPLE GLAZED LEG OF PORK

This recipe is not suitable to freeze or microwave.

1 leg of pork
1 teaspoon salt
⅓ cup honey
¼ cup light soya sauce
440g can crushed pineapple
1 tablespoon grated fresh ginger
¼ cup water
3 teaspoons cornflour

Ask butcher to score the pork rind well. Place pork in well-oiled baking dish. Rub salt well into rind. Bake in hot oven 30 minutes or until rind starts to crackle. Reduce heat to moderate, continue cooking until pork is well browned and tender. (Allow about 25 minutes per 500g cooking time.)

When pork is cooked, pour combined honey, soya sauce, undrained pineapple and ginger over pork. Cook further 20 minutes, spooning sauce over occasionally. Remove pork from baking dish. Skim off excess fat which has formed on top of pan juices. Add blended water and cornflour to pan juices. Stir constantly over heat until sauce boils and thickens.

Pineapple Glazed Leg of Pork

Table: Appley Hoare Antiques; china: "Runnymede", Wedgwood

ABOVE: Ham and Pork Terrine. BELOW: Roast Beef with Fresh Herb Dressing

HAM AND PORK TERRINE

Terrine can be made up to a week before required. This recipe is not suitable to freeze or microwave.

500g thinly sliced ham or pork fat
250g pork rashers
500g pork and veal mince
2 tablespoons madeira
2 eggs
½ teaspoon ground coriander
½ teaspoon ground allspice (pimento)
½ teaspoon dried tarragon leaves
¼ teaspoon ground nutmeg
¼ teaspoon ground cinnamon
pinch ground cardamom
pinch ground marjoram
250g sliced leg ham, chopped

Line sides and base of 14cm x 21cm loaf pan with thin slices of fat. Remove rind from pork, chop rashers roughly, then process until roughly minced. Add pork and veal mince, madeira, eggs and spices and process ingredients until smooth.

Spoon one-third of the pork mixture into loaf pan, top with half the ham.

Repeat layering, ending with pork mixture. Cover with foil. Place in baking dish with enough hot water to come halfway up sides of pan. Bake in moderate oven for 1½ hours. Cool, refrigerate overnight before slicing.

ROAST BEEF WITH FRESH HERB DRESSING

Prepare dressing several hours before using. Beef can be cooked up to 2 days ahead of serving. This recipe is not suitable to freeze or microwave.

1kg beef eye fillet
1 tablespoon whole black peppercorns, coarsely crushed
30g butter
2 tablespoons oil
FRESH HERB DRESSING
1 tablespoon chopped parsley
1 tablespoon chopped fresh chives
3 green shallots, chopped
2 teaspoons chopped fresh tarragon (or ½ teaspoon dried tarragon leaves)
1 teaspoon capers, chopped
2 teaspoons drained canned green peppercorns
½ teaspoon dry mustard
½ cup tarragon vinegar
½ cup oil
pinch sugar

Trim any sinew or fat from beef, tie into neat shape with string. Roll in peppercorns. Heat butter and oil in baking dish. Add beef to dish, cook over heat until well browned all over. Place dish in moderate oven, bake 45 minutes for medium rare or until cooked as required. Remove from oven, cool to room temperature. Remove string, slice beef thinly. Arrange beef on serving dish, top with dressing. Serve remaining dressing separately.

Fresh Herb Dressing: Combine parsley, chives, shallots, tarragon, capers, peppercorns and mustard in bowl. Stir in vinegar, oil and sugar.

Serves 4 to 6.

TRADITIONAL CHRISTMAS GLAZED LEG OF HAM

A golden, glistening ham, aside from being delicious, makes an impressive centrepiece for the Christmas table. Choose any of the following glazes for ham on the bone or canned hams.

Most people today prefer to buy a cooked ham which is ready to eat immediately. If it is to be glazed to make a more festive presentation, cooking time is only about 45 minutes.

However, if you have to bake an uncooked ham, wipe it well, wrap it loosely in foil, place fat side up (still retaining the rind) in a baking dish. Bake in moderately slow oven (allow about 20 minutes per 500g for hams up to 6kg and 15 minutes per 500g for larger hams). About 45 minutes before the end of the total cooking time, remove the foil; allow ham to cool slightly, then pull away the rind.

Alternatively, an uncooked ham can be covered with a scone dough. You'll need about 1kg of scone dough. Use 1kg self-raising flour sifted into a bowl with 1 teaspoon of salt. Add enough milk (about 3 or 4 cups) to give a soft sticky dough. Knead the dough lightly on a floured surface until smooth. Roll the dough to 1cm thickness, mould it around the ham. Place in well-greased baking dish; allow the same cooking times as above. Test with a skewer about 30 minutes before end of cooking time. When ham is tender, pull off and discard the dough, pull away rind.

To glaze the ham: Remove rind from ham, run thumb around edge of rind just under skin. Start pulling rind from widest edge of ham, using fingers to loosen it from the fat. When you have pulled it to within 15cm of shank end, take a very sharp pointed knife and cut through rind around shank end of leg in decorative pattern. Continue to pull the rind slowly and carefully away from the fat up to this decorative pattern.

With knife, cut across fat at about 5cm intervals; cut just through the surface of the top fat, not deeply, or the fat will spread apart during cooking instead of keeping a neat shape.

Put ham into large baking dish,

Traditional Christmas Glazed Leg of Ham

brush well with desired glaze. Bake in moderate oven 45 minutes. Brush glaze frequently over ham for best results. All the recipes for glazes can be made a week in advance if preferred. None of the glazes are suitable to freeze or microwave.

Canned ham: To glaze a canned ham, open can at both ends, push ham out into baking dish. Place in moderate oven a few minutes to allow jelly to melt. Pour this jelly mixture off, brush with any of the glazes given in our recipes. Bake in moderate oven for 15 to 20 minutes.

To store ham on the bone: Wrap loosely in a clean teatowel or pillowcase which has been rinsed in water and wrung out tightly. If you do this every day the ham will keep well. Store in refrigerator; the air must be able to circulate around the ham so do not have a tight covering. Do not store the ham in its original cheesecloth or plastic covering. Recommended maximum keeping time: 4 weeks.

To freeze: Ham can be frozen. Recommended maximum time: 2 months.

CITRUS LIQUEUR GLAZE

Cointreau and Grand Marnier are citrus-flavoured liqueurs.

1 orange
1 cup concentrated orange juice
¼ cup honey
¼ cup brown sugar
½ teaspoon dark soya sauce
1 teaspoon French mustard
2 tablespoons Cointreau or Grand Marnier

Remove rind from orange, remove any white pith. Cut rind into thin strips, drop into saucepan of boiling water, boil 3 minutes, drain.

Combine undiluted orange juice, honey, sugar, orange rind strips, soya sauce and mustard in a small saucepan, stir constantly over heat, without boiling, until sugar is dissolved. Remove from the heat, stir in liqueur. Cool before using.

MERRY CHRISTMAS

BRANDIED APRICOT GLAZE

1 cup apricot jam
½ teaspoon dark soya sauce
2 tablespoons brown vinegar
1 teaspoon dry mustard
¼ cup brandy
Sieve warmed jam, combine with remaining ingredients, mix well.

PINEAPPLE-ORANGE GLAZE

¼ cup canned pineapple juice
2 teaspoons dark soya sauce
2 tablespoons orange marmalade
1 tablespoon honey
¼ cup brown sugar
1 tablespoon brandy

Combine all ingredients in saucepan, stir constantly over heat until mixture boils, reduce heat, simmer uncovered 10 minutes. Cool before using.

CRANBERRY CURRANT GLAZE

Any left-over glaze can be stored in a screw-top jar in the refrigerator and served with hot or cold meats.

340g jar red currant jelly
290g jar cranberry sauce
2 tablespoons lemon juice
⅓ cup brandy
Combine jelly and cranberry sauce in saucepan, stir constantly over heat, without boiling, until jelly is melted and combined with sauce. Remove from heat, stir in lemon juice and brandy, strain before serving.

TROPICAL APRICOT GLAZE

Select a mild or hot chutney for this glaze, according to your taste.

½ cup apricot jam
¼ cup pawpaw and mango chutney
2 tablespoons brandy
⅓ cup water
2 teaspoons Worcestershire sauce
Combine jam, chutney, brandy, water and sauce in a saucepan, stir constantly over heat, without boiling, for 5 minutes. Strain liquid, cool before using.

HOW TO CARVE A HAM

A ham stand with prongs which secures the ham in position makes carving much easier. If using a stand, remove the pelvic, or jutting-out bone under the ham so it fits firmly on the stand. If a stand is not available, a pudding basin makes an excellent substitute.

1 Cut a circle in rind at top.

2 Run thumb or fingers around edge of ham, gently pull from the cut circle, removing rind. Leave rind attached to base of ham so that when enough ham has been cut, the rind can be replaced, keeping the ham moist.

3 To start carving, cut small wedge in top of ham and remove.

4 Take long sweeps of the knife to get long slices. As you carve, slices will increase in size.

5 Ham can be adjusted in basin to carve it from the side.

6 When carving is complete, pull rind back over ham, pressing it firmly in position; this prevents ham from drying on the surface.

FROSTED CHRISTMAS CAKE

Place cake on a prepared board. Use a 2 egg white quantity of fluffy frosting (see page 112) to cover the cake.

Decorate cake with holly. We made a tree from almond paste shaped into a cone (as shown). Place silver cachous on tree, use a little of the frosting to help them stick. Dust the tree with sifted icing sugar. Mould gift shapes

from marzipan, then paint them with food colouring. A double band of ribbon around the base looks quite effective to finish the cake.

CLASSIC CHRISTMAS CAKE

Cake can be covered in almond or marzipan paste; you will need 500g paste to cover a 20cm square or 23cm round cake. Knead the paste with a little sifted pure icing sugar until the paste loses its stickiness. Brush the cake liberally but evenly with lightly beaten egg white. Roll the paste out on a surface lightly dusted with icing sugar, large enough to cover the cake.

Lift the paste onto the cake with rolling pin, smooth out folds with sugared hands. Trim excess paste away. Leave cake to stand for a day if time permits. You will need 750g soft icing to cover the almond paste.

Brush the paste lightly but evenly

TOP: Frosted Christmas Cake. ABOVE: Classic Christmas Cake

MERRY CHRISTMAS

with egg white. Knead the icing with sifted pure icing sugar until it loses its stickiness. Roll out and apply to the cake in the same way as the almond paste. Trim edges, leave to stand a day for icing to firm.

Place the cake on a prepared board. Twist "sausages" of soft icing to make a pretty edging for the cake. We used twisted cord and bought decorations to make the cake look attractive.

AUSTRALIAN CHRISTMAS CAKE

You will need a 200g roll of marzipan or almond paste for the top of this cake.

Place cake on a prepared board. Glaze the top of the cake with about 2 tablespoons warmed, sieved apricot jam. Roll the almond paste out on a surface dusted with sifted icing sugar to the same size as the top of the cake, trim to size using the cake pan used for the cake as a guide. Pinch a frill around the edge. Decorate with dried flowers; we used pine cones, gumnuts and wattle. A double band of ribbon finishes off the side of the cake. Store the cake in an airtight container.

SIMPLE CHRISTMAS CAKE

Place the cake on a prepared board, frost the top with a 1 egg white quantity of fluffy frosting (see page 112) to represent snow. Secure a paper frill around the cake with sticky tape. Decorate with bought decorations.

Dresser: Wentworth Antiques; china: "Colleen", Royal Doulton

ABOVE:
Australian
Christmas
Cake
LEFT: Simple
Christmas
Cake

Dresser: Wentworth Antiques; linen: Studio Haus

IRRESISTIBLE NIBBLES
·NIBBLES·
To Have With Drinks

*Instead of a lavish dinner, have a drinks party and serve
tempting savouries. Best of all, much of the preparation can
be done ahead. Allow about 5 savouries per person.*

Curry Dip

CURRY DIP

Seafood can be prepared and vegetables blanched up to 12 hours before the party. The dip can be made up to 24 hours before required. Blanch vegetables in order of time they take to soften, for example, beans will take the longest and snow peas the shortest. To blanch vegetables, drop them into a saucepan of boiling water, return to the boil, drain. Place vegetables into bowl of iced water to regain colour and retain crispness. This recipe is not suitable to freeze.

350g jar thick mayonnaise
3 teaspoons curry powder
2 teaspoons chilli sauce
2 teaspoons lemon juice
⅓ cup sour cream
½ teaspoon Worcestershire sauce
3 green shallots, finely chopped

Combine ingredients in a bowl, mix well. Serve as a dip with fresh seafood and vegetables. We chose prawns, blanched beans, broccoli, snow peas, carrots and yellow beans or substitute other vegetables.

Makes about 1½ cups.

MINI PATE STRUDELS

We used Grand Marnier pâté but any favourite pâté can be used. This recipe is not suitable to freeze or microwave.

15g butter
250g baby mushrooms, sliced
250g pâté
1 egg, lightly beaten
⅔ cup packaged breadcrumbs
⅓ cup sour cream
¼ cup chopped parsley
5 sheets fillo pastry
60g butter, melted, extra

Heat butter in saucepan, add mushrooms, cook, covered, until soft. Beat pâté in bowl until soft, stir in mushroom mixture, egg, breadcrumbs, sour cream and parsley. Brush half of one sheet of pastry with extra butter, fold in half, brush with butter. Place one-fifth of the pâté mixture down folded edge of pastry, fold in sides, roll up, place on oven tray. Repeat with remaining pastry, butter and pâté mixture. Brush strudels with butter, bake in moderately hot oven for about 15 minutes or until golden brown. Cut diagonally into 3cm pieces.

Makes about 30.

TROPICAL SCALLOP SAVOURIES

Prepare savouries on toothpicks as close to serving time as possible. This recipe is not suitable to freeze.

¼ cup fresh orange juice
¼ cup French dressing
½ teaspoon seeded mustard
12 large scallops, halved
2 bananas, sliced
6 bacon rashers

From left: Mini Pâté Strudels; Tropical Scallop Savouries; Chicken and Ham Croquettes; Mini Crab Tartlets; Devilled Toast Squares

Combine orange juice, dressing and mustard in shallow dish; add scallops, marinate for 1 hour.

Cut bananas into 24 pieces. Grill or microwave bacon until it is limp. Cut each rasher into 4 strips. Wrap a strip around scallop and banana, secure with a toothpick. Grill or microwave savouries until bacon is crisp, basting scallops frequently with remaining orange marinade.

Makes 24.

CHICKEN AND HAM CROQUETTES

Croquettes can be made completely and kept refrigerated for about 3 days. They can be frozen for up to 1 month. Thaw before using or they spatter when cooked and the crumbs darken before the croquettes are heated through. This recipe is not suitable to microwave.

½ barbecued chicken
125g ham
1 chicken stock cube, crumbled
1 onion, finely chopped
1 cup grated tasty cheese
½ cup dry instant potato
1½ cups boiling water
1 egg, lightly beaten
½ cup milk
2 cups packaged breadcrumbs
oil for deep frying

Remove skin and bones from chicken; mince or process chicken and ham until fine, mix in stock cube, onion and cheese. Place potato in bowl, add water, stir until well mixed.

Combine meat mixture and potato. Roll mixture into croquette shapes about 5cm long. Dip croquettes in combined egg and milk, roll in breadcrumbs. Repeat egg and breadcrumbs for best results. Refrigerate uncovered, 1 hour. Deep fry in hot oil until golden brown and heated through.

Makes about 50.

MINI CRAB TARTLETS

Pastry cases can be prepared for baking up to a day ahead. Fill just before baking. This recipe is not suitable to freeze or microwave.

3 sheets frozen ready-rolled
    wholemeal pastry
2 bacon rashers, chopped
2 small zucchini, grated
185g can crab, drained
1 teaspoon lemon juice
2 tablespoons chopped fresh dill (or
    ½ teaspoon dried dill tips)
½ cup thickened cream
2 eggs, lightly beaten

Line 24 small, deep patty pans with pastry, cut out with an 8cm cutter. Cook bacon in frying pan (or microwave) until crisp, drain on absorbent paper. Add zucchini to the pan, cook few minutes over high heat until soft, remove from heat. Stir in crab, lemon juice, dill, cream, eggs and bacon; mix

well. Fill pastry cases three-quarters full with crab mixture. Bake in a moderately hot oven for 5 minutes, reduce heat to moderate, bake further 10 minutes or until filling has set and pastry browned. Serve immediately.

Makes 24.

DEVILLED TOAST SQUARES

Mini Toast Squares are an imported product, obtainable from delicatessens and gourmet sections of supermarkets. Topping can be prepared several hours before using. This recipe is not suitable to freeze or microwave.

30g butter
½ cup slivered almonds
2 tablespoons chutney
¼ teaspoon chilli powder
½ cup grated tasty cheese
80g packet Mini Toast Squares

Melt butter in saucepan, add almonds and stir over heat until lightly browned, drain on absorbent paper. Transfer almonds to bowl, stir in chutney, chilli and cheese. Spread mixture on pieces of toast, grill until golden brown.

Makes about 24.

CUCUMBER WITH DILL AND GARLIC

Cream cheese topping can be made a day before required. This recipe is not suitable to freeze.

250g packet cream cheese, softened
1 tablespoon chopped fresh dill (or
    ¼ teaspoon dried dill tips)
2 cloves garlic, crushed
1 tablespoon plain yoghurt
1 long green thin cucumber

Beat cream cheese in small bowl with electric mixer until smooth, beat in dill, garlic and yoghurt. Cut cucumber into 1cm slices, spread with cream cheese mixture, top with pieces of canned pimiento if desired.

Makes about 20.

MORTADELLA WEDGES

Use mortadella slices 12cm wide. Prepare up to 12 hours before required. Keep covered tightly in refrigerator or wedges will dry out. This recipe is not suitable to freeze.

125g packet cream cheese,
    softened
¼ cup milk
1 tablespoon French onion soup mix
20 slices mortadella

Beat cream cheese, milk and soup mix together in small bowl with electric

mixer until smooth. Sandwich 5 slices of mortadella with a quarter of the cream cheese mixture spread between each slice. Cut into 8 wedges, top with slices of gherkin, rockmelon, olive or pickled onion if desired. Repeat with remaining ingredients; refrigerate until ready to serve.

Makes 32.

TABBOULEH TOMATOES

Prepare tabbouleh the day before required and keep covered in refrigerator. Fill tomatoes up to several hours before serving. Italian parsley is the flat-leafed variety. This recipe is not suitable to freeze.

20 large cherry tomatoes
¼ cup cracked wheat
½ cup chopped Italian parsley
2 tablespoons chopped fresh mint
3 green shallots, finely chopped
1 tablespoon lemon juice
1 tablespoon oil

Cut top from each tomato, scoop out pulp, reserve for another use. Soak wheat in hot water for 20 minutes; drain well.

Combine wheat, parsley, mint, shallots, lemon juice and oil in bowl; mix well. Spoon tabbouleh into tomatoes, refrigerate, covered.

Makes 20.

SALMON HERBED PIKELETS

Pikelets can be made in advance and frozen in a single layer when cold. The topping is not suitable to freeze. The topping can be made the day before if desired. This recipe is not suitable to microwave.

1 cup self-raising flour
¼ teaspoon bicarbonate of soda
⅔ cup buttermilk
1 egg, lightly beaten
15g butter, melted
2 tablespoons chopped parsley
1 tablespoon chopped fresh chives
TOPPING
185g packaged cream cheese
1 tablespoon lemon juice
220g can red salmon, drained
1 tablespoon chopped fresh chives

Sift flour and soda into bowl, stir in combined buttermilk, egg, butter, parsley and chives, mix to a smooth batter (or process until smooth). Drop dessertspoons of batter into hot greased frying pan. Cook one side until light golden brown, turn, cook other side. Cool on wire rack. Pipe topping onto pikelets, sprinkle with chives.

Topping: Blend or process cheese, lemon juice and salmon until smooth.

Makes about 24.

Top, from centre: Tabbouleh Tomatoes; Cucumber with Dill and Garlic; Salmon Herbed Pikelets; bottom: Mortadella Wedges

21

SMOKED EEL AND CHIVE SPREAD

Spread can be made 2 days ahead. Spread onto bread as close to serving time as possible. This recipe is not suitable to freeze.

185g smoked eel
90g butter, softened
⅔ cup sour cream
1 tablespoon mayonnaise
1 tablespoon lemon juice
½ teaspoon Worcestershire sauce
1 tablespoon chopped fresh chives

Skin and bone eel. Blend or process eel and butter until smooth. Add sour cream, mayonnaise, lemon juice and Worcestershire sauce. Process until combined. Push through a sieve, stir in half the chives. Spread on buttered pumpernickel or rye bread. Sprinkle with remaining chives.

STUFFED MUSHROOMS

Choose small even-sized mushrooms about 2cm in diameter. Mushrooms can be prepared a day before required. Bake just before serving. This recipe is not suitable to freeze or microwave.

375g mushrooms
2 bacon rashers, chopped
¼ cup grated tasty cheese
¼ teaspoon French mustard
1 cup stale breadcrumbs
1 egg, lightly beaten
¼ cup milk
1 tablespoon chopped parsley
2 slices tasty cheese, extra
1 tomato

Remove stems from mushrooms. Cook bacon in frying pan until crisp. Remove from heat, stir in grated cheese, mustard and breadcrumbs. Stir in egg, milk and parsley, fill stuffing into mushrooms. Cut extra cheese slices into 1cm squares, slice tomato, then cut each slice into 8 small segments. Place a square of cheese on top of each mushroom; top with a segment of tomato. Place stuffed mushrooms on oven trays; bake in moderately hot oven for about 8 minutes, or until cheese is melted.

SALMON BOATS

Filling can be made up to a day before required. Fill boats just before heating. This recipe is not suitable to freeze or microwave.

1 bacon rasher, finely chopped
2 green shallots, finely chopped
220g can red salmon, drained
¼ cup grated tasty cheese
1 tablespoon mayonnaise
¼ cup cream
2 packets pastry boats
2 tablespoons grated parmesan cheese

Cook bacon in frying pan (or microwave) until crisp. Add shallots, mix well, remove from heat. Stir in salmon, tasty cheese, mayonnaise and cream. Fill pastry boats with salmon mixture, place on oven tray, sprinkle with parmesan cheese. Bake in moderate oven 10 minutes or until heated through.
Makes 24.

CHEESE AND PIMIENTO ROUNDS

Topping can be made about 12 hours before serving. Bread can be toasted several days ahead; store in refrigerator or freeze for a month. Topping is not suitable to freeze.

12 slices bread
60g butter, melted
30g butter, extra
1 onion, chopped
190g can sweet red pimientos, drained, chopped
¾ cup grated tasty cheese
2 tablespoons chopped parsley
1 tablespoon mayonnaise
2 bacon rashers, finely chopped

Cut 2 x 5cm rounds from each slice of bread. Brush both sides of rounds with butter. Place on oven tray, bake in moderate oven for about 10 minutes or until golden brown, cool.

Melt extra butter in saucepan, add onion, cook until onion is soft. Place onion in bowl, stir in pimientos, cheese, parsley and mayonnaise. Cook bacon in frying pan (or microwave) until crisp, add to cheese mixture. Spread over toast, place on oven tray, bake in moderate oven for about 5 minutes or until heated through.
Makes 24.

PRAWN PATE CURLS

Prawns can be prepared for frying several hours before required. Buy or make your own pâté. This recipe is not suitable to freeze or microwave.

24 medium uncooked prawns
185g pâté
1 egg white, lightly beaten
stale breadcrumbs
oil for deep-frying

Shell prawns, leaving tails intact, remove back vein. With sharp knife cut deeply along back of prawns, do not cut right through. Gently press prawns out flat with side of knife. Place a teaspoonful of pâté onto centre of cut side of flattened out prawn. Roll prawn up to enclose pâté. Brush prawn curls with egg white, coat with breadcrumbs. Deep-fry prawns in hot oil for about a minute or until golden brown and just tender. Drain on absorbent paper, serve immediately.
Makes 24.

MARINATED SALAMI AND TOMATO SAVOURIES

This recipe is not suitable to freeze.

125g thinly sliced salami
⅓ cup oil
2 tablespoons lemon juice
½ teaspoon dried oregano leaves
1 clove garlic, crushed
1½ tablespoons chopped parsley
1 small breadstick, sliced
butter
2 ripe tomatoes, sliced

Top: Stuffed Mushrooms; bottom: Smoked Eel and Chive Spread

Clockwise from top left: Marinated Salami and Tomato Savouries; Cheese and Pimiento Rounds; Salmon Boats; Prawn Pâté Curls; Mini Party Quiches

Place salami in bowl and stir in combined oil, lemon juice, oregano, garlic and 1 tablespoon of parsley. Stand 2 hours or overnight.

Place a slice of salami on each slice of bread, top with quartered slices of tomatoes, sprinkle lightly with remaining parsley.

Makes about 24.

MINI PARTY QUICHES

Fillings can be made a day before required. Each filling is enough for 36 pastry cases. Pastry cases can be frozen for up to a month. Fillings are not suitable to freeze. This recipe is not suitable to microwave.

375g packet fillo pastry
melted butter or oil
SPINACH FILLING
250g packet frozen spinach
1 bacon rasher, chopped
1 small onion, chopped
125g cottage cheese
1 egg, lightly beaten
⅔ cup thickened cream
ASPARAGUS FILLING
1 bacon rasher, chopped
310g can asparagus cuts, drained
2 green shallots, chopped
½ cup grated tasty cheese
1 egg, lightly beaten
⅔ cup thickened cream
MUSHROOM FILLING
1 bacon rasher, chopped
125g mushrooms, chopped
1 tablespoon chopped fresh chives
1 tablespoon chopped parsley
½ cup grated tasty cheese
1 egg, lightly beaten
⅔ cup thickened cream

Use 6 layers of fillo pastry at a time for making the quiches (there are about 24 layers in each 375g packet of pastry). Brush between each layer with melted butter or oil. Keep pastry covered with greaseproof paper, then a damp cloth when exposed to the air.

Use a sharp 6cm cutter to cut 36 rounds from buttered sheets of pastry, place rounds into shallow round-based patty pans, fill with desired filling. Bake in moderate oven 15 minutes or until golden brown; cool.

Spinach Filling: Press out as much liquid from thawed spinach as possible. Cook bacon and onion in frying pan until bacon is crisp; drain on absorbent paper. Combine spinach, bacon mixture and sieved cottage cheese in bowl, mix well. Place a teaspoonful of the filling into each pastry case, top with a teaspoon of the combined egg and cream.

Asparagus Filling: Cook bacon in frying pan until crisp; drain on absorbent paper. Combine bacon in bowl with asparagus, shallots and cheese. Place a teaspoonful of the mixture into each pastry case, top with a teaspoon of the combined egg and cream.

Mushroom Filling: Cook bacon in frying pan (or microwave) until crisp; add mushrooms, cook few minutes and add chives, parsley and cheese. Place a teaspoonful of the mixture into each pastry case, top with a teaspoon of the combined egg and cream.

COD AND BASIL BEARNAISE PATE

Pâté can be made, covered and refrigerated up to 2 days before required. This recipe is not suitable to freeze.

500g smoked cod
¼ cup white vinegar
3 egg yolks
125g butter, melted
1 tablespoon chopped fresh basil
1 green shallot, chopped
2 teaspoons gelatine
2 tablespoons water

Place smoked cod in frying pan, add enough water to just cover. Cover pan, bring to the boil, reduce heat, simmer 5 minutes. Drain, flake cod with fork, cool (or microwave on HIGH for about 5 minutes).

Place vinegar in saucepan, bring to the boil, boil until reduced to about half, cool to room temperature. Blend or process vinegar and egg yolks for 30 seconds. With motor operating, gradually add hot, bubbling butter; add basil, blend until basil is finely chopped. Transfer to bowl, stir in shallot and cod.

Combine gelatine with water, dissolve over hot water (or microwave on HIGH about 20 seconds). Add to cod mixture, pour into serving dish, refrigerate several hours or until firm.

Makes about 2 cups.

MUSHROOM PORT PATE

Make up to a week in advance if desired and store covered in the refrigerator. This recipe is not suitable to freeze.

500g chicken livers
125g butter
1 small onion, finely chopped
125g mushrooms, sliced
2 cloves garlic, crushed
250g lean ham, chopped
½ cup port
300ml carton thickened cream

Clean and trim livers, chop coarsely. Heat butter in saucepan, add onion, cook until onion is soft (or microwave on HIGH for about 3 minutes). Add mushrooms, garlic, livers, ham and port. Cook, stirring, 10 minutes (or microwave on HIGH for about 5 minutes, or until livers are tender). Blend

Clockwise from left: Tuna and Anchovy Pâté; Mushroom Port Pâté; Cod and Basil Bearnaise Pâté

or process liver mixture with cream until smooth. Pour into serving dish, refrigerate several hours or until firm.

Makes about 3 cups.

TUNA AND ANCHOVY PATE

Pâté can be made up to 2 days in advance; store covered in refrigerator. This recipe is not suitable to freeze.

425g can tuna, drained
75g can anchovy fillets, drained
2 tablespoons drained capers
2 egg yolks
¼ cup olive oil
2 tablespoons lemon juice
200g carton sour cream
2 tablespoons chopped parsley

Blend or process tuna, anchovy fillets, capers, egg yolks, oil and lemon juice until smooth, add sour cream and parsley, blend until combined. Spoon into serving dish, cover and refrigerate overnight.

Makes about 2 cups.

24

6 Menus For
·SPECIAL·
OCCASIONS

Choosing a successful menu for a large family or formal gathering can be difficult. In this section we have created 6 menus which are sure to prove popular. A sumptuous seafood dinner, a flavoursome curry with spicy accompaniments, light and luscious salads, delicious pâtés and irresistible desserts and punches can all be adapted to suit any special occasion.

Top, from left: Seafood Christmas Dinner for 6; Picnic for 8;
Curry Party for 6. Bottom, from left: Celebration Lunch for 15;
Casual Buffet for 12; New Year's Party for 10

1 SEAFOOD CHRISTMAS DINNER FOR 6

We are fortunate to have access to some wonderful seafood, and in our hot climate, it makes a change from the traditional Christmas dinner. Buy fresh seafood which is in season, for the best flavours and buy it as close to serving time as possible.

DUCK TERRINE

Terrine is at its best made 2 days ahead of serving. This recipe is not suitable to freeze or microwave.

No. 15 duck
250g veal steak
90g pork or ham fat
125g chicken livers
30g butter
1 small onion, chopped
1 clove garlic, crushed
1 egg, lightly beaten
1 tablespoon port
¼ teaspoon dried thyme leaves
3 bay leaves
125g pork or ham fat, extra

Remove skin, fat and bones from duck; chop all meat roughly. Trim veal and chop roughly.

Process duck meat, veal, fat and livers until smooth. Combine in large bowl, mix well.

Melt butter in saucepan, add onion and garlic, cook until onion is soft. Add to meat mixture with egg, port, and thyme; mix well. Place bay leaves on base of 3 cup capacity ovenproof dish, line base and sides with thin slices of extra fat. Reserve a few slices for top. Spread terrine mixture into dish, press down firmly, top with reserved fat. Cover with foil, secure with string.

Place in baking dish with enough hot water to come halfway up sides of dish. Bake in moderate oven for 1½ hours. Cool, cover, refrigerate with a weight on top.

Serve with Melba Toast.

MELBA TOAST

Melba toast will keep well for about 2 weeks if stored in an air tight container. This recipe is not suitable to freeze or microwave.

Remove all crusts from square loaf of unsliced bread. Cut bread in half. Cut each loaf diagonally in half, giving 4 thick triangular-shaped pieces of bread. Cut into thin slices using an electric or serrated knife.

Place triangles in single layer on un-greased oven trays. Bake in moderate oven for about 15 minutes or until lightly browned. Turn frequently during the cooking time.

SEAFOOD PLATTER

This selection of seafood is only a guide, choose whatever you prefer or what is at its best at the time.

2 x 750g cooked lobsters
12 cooked king prawns, shelled
18 oysters
2 cooked mud crabs
12 mussels
6 slices smoked salmon
50g jar red caviar
lemon juice
1 small white onion, sliced
lemon wedges
capers
1 avocado
French dressing
watercress or parsley

Cut lobsters in half lengthways; using fingers, ease meat out of tails in one piece. Wash 2 of the shells, slice meat, toss in lemon juice, return meat to the 2 shells. Arrange lobster on serving platter with prawns, sprinkle a little red caviar on each oyster, place on platter.

With small knife, gently cut away grey fibrous tissue underneath crabs. Rinse to clean inside of crab. Cut off claws and big nippers. Crack nippers lightly with back of cleaver or knife to break through the hard shell: this makes it easier to eat. Cut crabs in half, then chop across each half 3 times. Arrange crab on platter.

Roll up salmon, place on serving platter, garnish with capers and onion rings; place cooked mussels on platter. Decorate platter with lemon wedges, avocado tossed in French dressing and watercress or parsley.

To cook mussels: Scrub mussels under cold water, remove beards. Place mussels in saucepan, add 1 cup water and 1 roughly chopped onion. Cover, bring to the boil, boil 1 minute or until shells open. Discard any unopened mussels. Place mussels in bowl, stir in ½ cup French dressing and sprinkle with some chopped parsley.

COCKTAIL SAUCE

We used a mild Chinese-style chilli sauce for this recipe. The sauce can be made several days before required. This sauce recipe is not suitable to freeze or microwave.

1 tablespoon oil
1 tablespoon grated fresh ginger
3 cloves garlic, crushed
¼ cup tomato sauce
¼ cup chilli sauce

1 SEAFOOD CHRISTMAS DINNER FOR 6

Duck Terrine with Melba Toast

Seafood Platter with Cocktail Sauce and Tartare Sauce

Peppercorn Salad

Tropical Fruit Bombe

Back, from left: Peppercorn Salad; Seafood

Platter; Tropical Fruit Bombe; centre: Melba Toast; front from left: Duck Terrine; Cocktail Sauce; Tartare Sauce

SPECIAL OCCASIONS

2 teaspoons sugar
1 tablespoon light soya sauce
2 teaspoons dry sherry
2 tablespoons water
½ cup cream

Place oil, ginger, garlic, tomato sauce and chilli sauce in saucepan. Stir over heat for 1 minute. Add sugar, soya sauce, sherry and water, bring slowly to the boil. Remove liquid from heat, cool to room temperature, stir cream into chilli mixture. Refrigerate until ready to serve.

Makes 1 cup.

TARTARE SAUCE

Sauce can be made a week before required. The mint is best added just before serving. This recipe is not suitable to freeze.

1 tablespoon capers, chopped
1 gherkin, chopped
1 tablespoon chopped fresh chives
1 teaspoon chopped fresh mint
½ cup mayonnaise
1 tablespoon lemon juice

Combine all ingredients in bowl.
Makes about 1 cup.

PEPPERCORN SALAD

1 lettuce
1 bunch endive
2 green shallots, chopped
1 tablespoon chopped parsley
1 clove garlic, crushed
¼ cup oil
½ teaspoon dried oregano leaves
2 tablespoons lemon juice
2 teaspoons drained canned green peppercorns
1 tablespoon French mustard

Wash lettuce and endive, dry well, tear roughly, place in salad bowl with shallots and parsley. Combine garlic with remaining ingredients in screw-top jar, shake well. Add to salad just before serving, toss lightly.

TROPICAL FRUIT BOMBE

Bombe can be made and frozen several days in advance.

60g unroasted macadamia nuts
1½ litres vanilla ice-cream
2 large ripe mangoes
½ cup sugar
⅔ cup water
2 teaspoons lemon juice
300ml carton thickened cream
PASSIONFRUIT SAUCE
6 passionfruit
2 tablespoons orange juice
2 tablespoons icing sugar
2 tablespoons Grand Marnier

Toast nuts on oven tray in moderate oven for about 5 minutes. Cool nuts to

2
PICNIC FOR 8

Marinated Olives
Sesame Chicken Rolls
Pineapple Beef Patties
Sate Pasta Salad
Tomato Basil Salad
Moist Banana Cake
Coconut Apple Slice

Back, from left: Tomato Basil Salad; Sate Pasta Salad; Coconut Apple Slice; centre,

room temperature, chop roughly.

Place ice-cream in large bowl, beat with a wooden spoon until just softened, fold in nuts. Spoon ice-cream into a 6 cup mould, press over base and up side of mould, leaving a hollow in the centre; cover with foil, freeze until firm. Blend or process mangoes until smooth: you will need 2 cups of mango purée. Place sugar and water in small saucepan, stir over heat, without boiling, until sugar is dissolved. Boil uncovered, without stirring, for about 5 minutes or until sugar syrup is thickened slightly; cool.

Combine mango, lemon juice and sugar syrup, pour into a shallow pan (a

lamington pan is ideal), cover with foil, freeze 1 hour or until just starting to harden around the edges. Beat cream until soft peaks form and fold in mango mixture in 2 lots. Return mango ice-cream to freezer, freeze until almost firm, beat well with a fork. Spoon ice-cream into hollow in mould, cover, freeze until firm.

To serve bombe: Dip mould into sink full of hot water for about 30 seconds, invert bombe onto serving dish. Return to freezer until firm. Decorate with fruit and serve with passionfruit sauce.

Passionfruit Sauce: Remove pulp from passionfruit into bowl, stir in remaining ingredients.

from left: Sesame Chicken Rolls; Pineapple Beef Patties; Moist Banana Cake; front: Marinated Olives

2 PICNIC FOR 8

This picnic food is easy to prepare; it is portable and we've included helpful hints for getting it all prepared ahead of time. Take along lots of drinks, both hot and cold, and a selection of fruit. Buy some freshly made breadrolls on the way and don't forget the butter.

MARINATED OLIVES

Prepare olives in advance: they will keep indefinitely if they are always covered with the liquid. Use a large jar, and, as the olives are used, simply add more olives. Keep airtight in cool dark place or in refrigerator. This recipe is not suitable to freeze.

250g black olives
250g green olives
½ cup lemon juice
1 cup olive oil
1 teaspoon French mustard
2 cloves garlic, crushed
¼ teaspoon dried oregano leaves
Combine all ingredients in jar; seal. Stand at least 24 hours before using.

SESAME CHICKEN ROLLS

Prepare up to a day before required, cool, cover and refrigerate. Slice before or at the picnic; they are delicious hot or cold. This recipe is not suitable to freeze.

16 chicken thighs
200g lean ham
125g large mushrooms
8 green shallots
2 tablespoons hoisin sauce
1 tablespoon light soya sauce
½ teaspoon sesame oil
1 tablespoon sesame seeds
Trim excess fat from chicken, cut thigh fillet from bone, leave skin intact. Cut ham, mushrooms and shallots into long thin strips. Combine sauces and oil, brush over inside of chicken fillets

and reserve remaining sauce for basting. Place the strips of ham, mushrooms and shallots in the centre of each fillet. Roll fillets and secure them with toothpicks.

Place on a rack over baking dish. Pour enough water in baking dish just to cover the base of the dish. Brush chicken with remaining sauce mixture, sprinkle with sesame seeds. Bake in moderately hot oven for about 40 minutes or until chicken is golden brown (or microwave on HIGH for about 15 minutes or until fillets are tender). Baste several times during cooking.

PINEAPPLE BEEF PATTIES

Prepare and cook up to 2 days before required. Keep refrigerated or freeze for up to a week. Serve cold with the sauce for dipping. This recipe is not suitable to microwave.

440g can crushed pineapple
500g topside mince
250g sausage mince
1 cup stale breadcrumbs
1 small green pepper, finely chopped
½ cup tomato sauce
1 teaspoon chilli sauce
plain flour
oil for shallow frying
SAUCE
½ cup mayonnaise
2 tablespoons tomato sauce
Drain pineapple, reserve ¼ cup syrup for the sauce. Combine pineapple, minces, breadcrumbs, pepper and sauces in bowl; mix well. Shape into 16 patties, coat lightly in flour, fry in hot oil until patties are browned both sides and cooked through.
Sauce: Combine mayonnaise, tomato sauce and reserved pineapple syrup.
Makes about 16.

SATE PASTA SALAD

Prepare pasta, vegetables and dressing up to a day before required. Combine pasta and vegetables up to several hours before required, add dressing just before serving. This recipe is not suitable to freeze.

500g packet spiral pasta
250g green beans
1 carrot
3 green shallots, sliced
1 stick celery, sliced
190g can champignons, drained, chopped
1 red pepper, finely chopped
60g (½ cup) roasted, unsalted peanuts
DRESSING
½ cup oil
¼ cup lemon juice

3
CURRY PARTY FOR 6

Spicy Tomato Puffs
Lamb Curry
Sambals
Custard Apple Ice-Cream with Ginger Sauce

3 tablespoons smooth peanut butter
1 teaspoon curry powder
Bring large saucepan of water to the boil, add pasta, boil rapidly uncovered for about 10 minutes or until pasta is just tender; drain. Cut beans in half lengthways, then into 5cm strips. Cut carrot into thin 5cm strips.

Bring saucepan of water to the boil, add beans, cook 2 minutes, add carrot, cook further 1 minute. Drain vegetables, rinse under cold water. Combine pasta and all vegetables with dressing; sprinkle with peanuts.
Dressing: Blend oil and lemon juice in a small bowl with peanut butter and curry powder.

TOMATO BASIL SALAD

Prepare up to 12 hours before required, keep covered in refrigerator. This recipe is not suitable to freeze.

4 tomatoes, peeled, sliced
2 cucumbers, sliced
1 onion, sliced
½ cup white vinegar
1 tablespoon chopped fresh basil (or 1 teaspoon dried basil leaves)
Layer vegetables in dish; sprinkle with combined vinegar and basil.

MOIST BANANA CAKE

Make cake the day before required. Store in airtight container when cold, or the cake can be frozen for up to a month. This recipe is not suitable to microwave.

250g soft butter
1 cup castor sugar
3 eggs
3 over-ripe bananas, finely mashed
2 cups self-raising flour
Cream butter and sugar in small bowl

Back, from left: Cauliflower Potato and Pepper Sambal; Tomato Onion Sambal; Lamb Curry; centre, left: Spicy Tomato Puffs; right: Salty Cinnamon Cashew Sambal; front, from left: Mango Mint Sambal; Cucumber Yoghurt Sambal; Custard Apple Ice-Cream with Ginger Sauce

with electric mixer until light and fluffy. Add eggs one at a time, beating well after each addition. Stir in bananas, then sifted flour. Pour into well greased 20cm baba or ring pan, bake in moderate oven for about 45 minutes. Stand a few minutes before turning cake onto wire rack to cool.

COCONUT APPLE SLICE

Slice can be prepared up to 2 days before required. Store in an airtight container in refrigerator or freeze up to a month. This recipe is not suitable to microwave.

90g butter
¼ cup castor sugar
1 egg yolk
¾ cup plain flour
¼ cup self-raising flour
½ cup apricot jam
½ x 410g can pie apple
½ teaspoon ground cinnamon
1½ cups coconut
50g (½ cup) roasted ground hazelnuts
⅓ cup castor sugar, extra
2 eggs

Cream butter, sugar and egg yolk in bowl with electric mixer until just combined, stir in sifted flours in 2 lots (this can be done in a food processor). Press mixture evenly over base of 19cm x 29cm lamington pan. Cover with greaseproof paper, sprinkle thickly with dried beans or rice, bake in moderately hot oven 10 minutes, remove paper and beans, bake further 5 minutes, cool 5 minutes. Spread base evenly with jam. Top with combined apple and cinnamon. Combine coconut, hazelnuts and extra sugar in bowl, beat in eggs with a fork. Crumble mixture over apples. Bake in moderately hot oven for about 30 minutes.

3 CURRY PARTY FOR 6

It doesn't have to be cold to have curry, it's a warm friendly meal at any time.

SPICY TOMATO PUFFS

Puffs can be prepared for baking about 12 hours ahead. Keep covered in refrigerator. This recipe is not suitable to freeze or microwave.

3 potatoes
1 tablespoon oil
1 teaspoon grated fresh ginger
2 tomatoes, peeled, chopped
½ teaspoon ground cumin
¼ teaspoon ground coriander
¼ teaspoon ground cardamom
¼ teaspoon turmeric
½ x 375g packet fillo pastry
60g butter, melted

Boil, steam or microwave potatoes until tender; drain, mash roughly.

Heat oil in saucepan. Add ginger, tomatoes, cumin, coriander, cardamom and turmeric. Cook, stirring, for 2 minutes. Add potato. Mix until combined; cool to room temperature.

Use a sheet of fillo pastry for each puff. Brush each sheet of pastry with butter, fold in half crossways. Place a tablespoonful of filling at one end of pastry. Fold sides of pastry over filling, roll up to enclose filling.

Repeat with remaining filling and pastry. Place puffs on greased oven tray, brush with butter. Bake in moderately hot oven 10 minutes, reduce heat to moderate, bake further 10 minutes or until golden brown.

LAMB CURRY

Lamb can be marinated a day ahead of cooking. The curry can be made 3 days ahead of serving, keep covered in refrigerator. Curry can be frozen for up to 2 months. This recipe is not suitable to microwave.

2½kg leg of lamb
1 tablespoon curry paste
1 teaspoon chilli powder
1 clove garlic, crushed
¼ cup brown vinegar
¼ teaspoon turmeric
60g ghee
2 onions, sliced
3 cloves garlic, crushed, extra
1 teaspoon grated fresh ginger
1 teaspoon ground coriander
½ teaspoon ground cumin
3 cups water
2 beef stock cubes, crumbled
1 tablespoon tomato paste
1 tablespoon cornflour
1 tablespoon water, extra

Trim excess fat from lamb, cut lamb into 2cm pieces. Place in bowl, mix in curry paste, chilli powder, garlic, vinegar and turmeric, cover, stand at least 30 minutes.

Heat half the ghee in frying pan, add half the lamb, stir constantly over high heat until well browned, place in bowl. Melt remaining ghee, add remaining lamb, stir until browned, return all lamb to the pan. Add onions, extra garlic, ginger, coriander and cumin, cook a few minutes, stirring constantly. Pour into ovenproof dish, add water, stock cubes and tomato paste, cover, bake in moderate oven 1 hour. Cool to room temperature, refrigerate overnight.

Next day, remove any fat from curry. Pour curry into large saucepan, bring to the boil, stir in blended cornflour and extra water. Stir constantly over heat until mixture boils and thickens.

4
CELEBRATION LUNCH FOR 15

Grand Marnier Pâté

Smoked Fish Savouries

Asparagus Strudel, Chicken Strudel, Seafood Strudel

Avocado and Olive Salad

Chocolate Cherry Liqueur Gateau

Clockwise from back right: Grand Marnier Pâté; Chicken Strudel; Seafood Strudel; Asparagus Strudel; Smoked Fish Savouries; Avocado and Olive Salad; far back: Cherry Liqueur Gateau

SAMBALS

Try these sambals with your curry. Also serve some chutney, mango is good, and any fresh or dried fruit, nuts and lime or lemon wedges. None of the sambals are suitable to freeze.

TOMATO ONION SAMBAL

Make a day ahead if preferred.

2 ripe tomatoes, peeled
1 onion, finely chopped
½ cup chopped parsley
Dice tomatoes, combine with onion and parsley; mix well.

CUCUMBER YOGHURT SAMBAL

Make a day ahead if preferred.

1 cucumber, peeled
1 teaspoon salt
200ml carton plain yoghurt
1 clove garlic, crushed
Slice cucumber thinly, place in bowl; sprinkle with salt, stand 30 minutes. Rinse cucumber under cold water; drain well. Combine yoghurt, garlic and cucumber, mix well.

CAULIFLOWER POTATO AND PEPPER SAMBAL

¼ cauliflower
1 cup water
1 teaspoon turmeric
2 potatoes, quartered
1 small red pepper, chopped
1 small green pepper, chopped
Cut cauliflower into flowerets. Bring water and turmeric to the boil in a saucepan, add potatoes and cauliflower, return to the boil, reduce heat, simmer, covered 15 minutes or until vegetables are just tender. Drain, cut potatoes into 2cm cubes. Place in large bowl, combine with cauliflower and peppers; mix gently with wooden spoon.
    Serve hot.

MANGO MINT SAMBAL

Make just before serving.

2 mangoes
1 tablespoon chopped fresh mint
Slice mangoes neatly, combine in bowl with mint.

SALTY CINNAMON CASHEW SAMBAL

Cashews can be prepared several days ahead, but they are delightful served hot from the pan.

1 teaspoon oil
185g (1½ cups) salted roasted cashews
½ cup sultanas
¼ teaspoon ground cinnamon
Heat oil in saucepan, add cashews and sultanas, stir constantly over heat for 2 minutes, mix in cinnamon.

CUSTARD APPLE ICE-CREAM WITH GINGER SAUCE

Prepare ice-cream up to a week ahead. Sauce can be made 2 days ahead.

1 teaspoon gelatine
2 teaspoons water
3 egg yolks
¼ cup castor sugar
½ cup milk
1 teaspoon vanilla essence
2 large ripe custard apples, seeded
300ml carton thickened cream
GINGER SAUCE
2 teaspoons grated fresh ginger
¼ cup brown sugar
1 cup water
1 tablespoon lemon juice
1 tablespoon water, extra
1½ teaspoons cornflour
1 tablespoon brandy
Sprinkle gelatine over water, dissolve over hot water. Whisk egg yolks and sugar together in heatproof bowl or in top of double saucepan, add milk and essence. Stir constantly over simmering water until custard thickens. Remove from heat, stir in gelatine mixture and 2 cups of mashed custard apples.
    Beat off the heat with rotary beater or electric mixer until custard becomes lukewarm. Fold in whipped cream. Pour ice-cream into loaf pan, cover with foil, freeze overnight. Serve with ginger sauce.
Ginger Sauce: Squeeze the juice from the ginger between 2 teaspoons. Combine water and sugar in small saucepan, stir constantly over heat without boiling, until sugar is dissolved. Bring to the boil, add ginger juice, lemon juice and blended extra water and cornflour. Stir constantly over heat until the sauce boils and thickens; stir in brandy.

4 CELEBRATION LUNCH FOR 15

A choice of 3 fillings is given for the strudels; each recipe makes 2 strudels. You will need 4 strudels to serve 15 people.

GRAND MARNIER PATE

Serve pâté with bread, toast, Melba Toast or crackers. Pâté is best prepared up to 2 days ahead, keep covered and refrigerated. Return to room temperature before serving. Grand Marnier is a citrus-flavoured liqueur. This recipe is not suitable to freeze.

500g chicken livers
⅓ cup Grand Marnier
90g butter
1 small onion, chopped
1 clove garlic, crushed
⅓ cup cream
¼ teaspoon ground nutmeg
½ teaspoon ground thyme
Trim and halve livers, place in bowl, with liqueur, stand 2 hours.
    Strain livers, reserve liquid. Melt half the butter in frying pan, add onion, garlic and livers, cook few minutes or until livers have changed in colour. Add reserved liquid, cook 1 minute. Blend or process mixture until smooth. Stir in remaining melted butter, cream, nutmeg and thyme. Pour into serving dish, cover, refrigerate.
    Makes about 2 cups.

SMOKED FISH SAVOURIES

Use smoked fish of your choice, we used smoked eel. Savouries can be prepared a day ahead and baked just before serving. This recipe is not suitable to freeze or microwave.

400g smoked fish
90g butter
6 green shallots, chopped
3 teaspoons plain flour
½ cup cream
½ teaspoon French mustard
2 tablespoons grated parmesan cheese
MUSTARD BUTTER
90g butter, softened
2 teaspoons Worcestershire sauce
few drops tabasco
½ teaspoon dry mustard
½ teaspoon French mustard
Place fish in frying pan, cover with water and bring to the boil, reduce heat, simmer, uncovered, 3 minutes each side or until easily flaked with fork. Remove from pan and drain; peel away skin and flake fish into bowl, removing any bones.
    Melt butter in saucepan, add shallots and flour, cook, stirring, for 1 minute. Add cream and mustard, stir constantly over heat until sauce boils and thickens slightly, stir into fish. Spread mustard butter onto toast or bread, spread with fish mixture, sprinkle with cheese. Place on oven trays, bake in moderate oven for about 10 minutes.
Mustard Butter: Combine all ingredients in bowl, beat until smooth.
    Makes about 35.

Chocolate Cherry Liqueur Gateau

mixture with sauce and parsley.

Lay 8 sheets fillo pastry on top of each other, brushing between each layer with oil. Spoon half of filling mixture down long edge of pastry, leaving about 5cm at each end. Roll up tightly to enclose the filling and tuck ends under. Repeat with remaining pastry and remaining filling. Place on oven trays, brush with oil. Bake in a moderate oven for about 30 minutes or until strudels are lightly browned.

ASPARAGUS STRUDEL

4 whole black peppercorns
1 green shallot
1½ cups milk
2 x 340g cans asparagus cuts
60g butter
¼ cup plain flour
1 cup grated tasty cheese
30g butter, extra
2 onions, thinly sliced
125g mushrooms, chopped
¼ cup sour cream
1 egg, lightly beaten
375g packet fillo pastry
½ cup oil
2 tablespoons grated parmesan cheese

Combine peppercorns, shallot and milk in saucepan. Gradually bring to the boil, remove from heat, cover, stand 5 minutes.

Drain asparagus, reserve ½ cup of liquid. Melt butter in saucepan, add flour, stir until smooth. Cook 1 minute. Gradually stir in strained milk, then reserved asparagus liquid and tasty cheese. Stir over heat until sauce boils and thickens.

Heat extra butter in saucepan, add onions, cook, stirring, until soft. Add mushrooms, cook until soft, stir in sour cream, asparagus, sauce and egg.

Lay 8 sheets of fillo pastry on top of each other, brush between each layer with oil. Spoon half the filling down long edge of pastry, leaving about 5cm at each end. Roll up tightly, enclose filling, tuck ends under. Place on oven tray, brush with oil, sprinkle with parmesan cheese. Repeat with remaining pastry and filling. Bake in a moderate oven for 30 minutes or until pastry is lightly browned.

CHICKEN STRUDEL

No. 15 chicken
1 small onion, sliced
1 stick celery, chopped
45g butter
4 green shallots, chopped
4 bacon rashers, chopped
2½ tablespoons plain flour
1 cup milk

SEAFOOD STRUDEL

Strudels can be prepared 2 weeks ahead and frozen, uncooked. To cook, put into moderate oven in their frozen state, allow longer cooking time, about 45 to 60 minutes overall cooking time. These recipes are not suitable to microwave.

500g uncooked king prawns
250g scallops
1½ cups water
½ cup dry white wine
1 small onion, chopped
60g butter
¼ cup plain flour
½ cup cream
30g butter, extra
4 green shallots, chopped
185g can crab, drained
2 tablespoons chopped parsley
375g packet fillo pastry
½ cup oil

Shell prawns, remove back veins, roughly chop prawns; reserve prawn shells. Clean scallops, cut in half. Place reserved prawn shells, water, wine and onion in saucepan, bring to the boil; reduce heat, simmer uncovered 5 minutes; drain, reserve stock. (You will need 1¼ cups stock.)

Heat butter in separate saucepan, add flour, stir until smooth, cook 1 minute. Remove from heat, gradually add reserved stock and cream, stir until smooth. Return to heat, stir until sauce boils and thickens, cool. Heat extra butter in small frying pan, add shallots and scallops, cook 1 minute, stir in prawns and crab, combine seafood

¼ cup sour cream
250g mushrooms, sliced
375g packet fillo pastry
½ cup oil
Combine chicken, onion and celery in saucepan with enough water to cover chicken. Bring to the boil, reduce heat, simmer covered 45 minutes. Remove chicken from stock, remove skin, remove chicken meat from bones, chop meat roughly.

Melt butter in frying pan, add shallots and bacon, cook, stirring, until bacon is soft. Add flour, stir until smooth, cook 1 minute. Gradually stir in milk, stir constantly over heat until mixture boils and thickens, stir in sour cream, mushrooms and chicken, cool.

Lay 8 sheets of fillo pastry on top of each other, brushing between each layer with oil. Spoon half the filling mixture down long edge of pastry, leaving about 5cm at each end. Roll up tightly to enclose filling, tuck ends under. Place on oven tray and brush with oil. Repeat with remaining pastry and remaining filling. Bake in a moderate oven for about 30 minutes or until lightly browned.

AVOCADO AND OLIVE SALAD

Salad greens can be prepared a day ahead, wash and dry, put into plastic bag, refrigerate.

1 lettuce
1 bunch endive
1 avocado, sliced
60g pitted black olives
½ cup oil
¼ cup white vinegar
¼ teaspoon dry mustard
1 teaspoon French mustard
Wash lettuce and endive, dry well, tear roughly and place in salad bowl with avocado and olives. Combine remaining ingredients; mix well. Pour over salad just before serving; toss lightly.

CHOCOLATE CHERRY LIQUEUR GATEAU

This cake can be made 2 days ahead; the filling can be put in the day before, and the final covering and decoration done on the day required. Unfilled cake can be frozen for up to 2 months. This recipe is not suitable to microwave.

1 packet chocolate butter cake mix
680g jar pitted Morello cherries
3 teaspoons cornflour
2 x 300ml cartons thickened cream
2 tablespoons Cherry Brandy
90g dark chocolate
1 small jar maraschino cherries (with stems)
1 egg white

5
CASUAL BUFFET FOR 12
Creamy Salmon Pâté
Smoky Cheese and Pumpkin Mini Quiches
Chicken and Leek Pie
Lamb in Red Wine Sauce
Stir-Fried Vegetables with Almonds
Fruity Brown Rice
Ham and Chutney Breadsticks
Chocolate Rum Sponge
Frozen Mango Mousse
Lemon Chocolate Squares

castor sugar
CHOCOLATE CREAM
½ cup thickened cream
125g dark chocolate, chopped
15g butter
Make cake mix as directed on packet. Pour mixture into deep greased 23cm round cake pan. Bake in moderate oven for about 35 minutes. Turn onto wire rack to cool.

Drain cherries, reserve syrup. Place cherries in saucepan. Blend cornflour with ⅓ cup of the reserved syrup, stir into cherries. Stir constantly over heat until mixture boils and thickens, cool to room temperature.

Cut cake into 3 layers. Place 1 layer on serving plate, brush with a little reserved cherry syrup, spread cherry mixture over cake. Top with another layer of cake, brush with a little more reserved syrup, spread with chocolate cream. Brush remaining layer with reserved syrup and place on top of chocolate cream; refrigerate 15 minutes. Combine cream and Cherry Brandy, beat until firm peaks form.

Spread three-quarters of the cream

Back, from left: Ham and Chutney Breadsticks; Fruity Brown Rice; Frozen Mango Mousse; centre, from left: Lamb in Red Wine Sauce; Chocolate Rum Sponge; Lemon Chocolate Squares; front, from left: Smoky Cheese and Pumpkin Mini Quiches; Creamy Salmon Pâté; Chicken and Leek Pie; Stir-fried Vegetables with Almonds

all over cake. Pipe around edge of cake with remaining cream. Decorate with chocolate leaves and frosted maraschino cherries. Refrigerate until ready to serve.

Chocolate Cream: Combine chocolate and cream in saucepan, stir over heat without boiling until chocolate is melted. Cool a few minutes and stir in butter. Refrigerate mixture until cold. Place chocolate mixture into small bowl of electric mixer, beat on medium speed until cream thickens.

Chocolate Leaves: Brush the backs of clean dry leaves evenly with a little melted chocolate and refrigerate until leaves are set. Peel the leaves away from the chocolate.

Frosted Cherries: Drain cherries and place cherries on absorbent paper; stand for 10 minutes.

Brush cherries lightly with egg white, then roll in castor sugar. Place on clean absorbent paper. Repeat rolling in sugar several times at 5 minute intervals until cherries are well sugar-coated. Place on cake as late as possible as sugar will dissolve.

 CASUAL BUFFET FOR 12

There are times when you feel like having a crowd of friends around, but don't want the formality of a sit-down dinner. This menu is easy to prepare and most of it can be done in advance. Serve the savouries with drinks. Give your guests a choice of 2 main courses and 3 accompaniments.

SPECIAL OCCASIONS

CREAMY SALMON PATE

Prepare pâté and toast up to several days ahead. Freeze the toast, refrigerate the covered pâté. This recipe is not suitable to microwave.

220g can red salmon, drained
185g packaged cream cheese,
softened
½ cup sour cream
1 tablespoon capers, drained
1 tablespoon lemon juice
24 slices bread
fresh dill
¼ red pepper, finely chopped
1 lemon
Blend or process salmon until smooth, add chopped cream cheese, sour cream, capers and lemon juice, process until smooth. Pour into serving bowl, refrigerate 1 hour or until set.

Cut 2 rounds from each slice of bread, place onto oven trays, bake in moderate oven 15 minutes or until bread is crisp. Serve toast spread with pâté; garnish with dill, red pepper and tiny wedges of lemon.

Makes 48.

SMOKY CHEESE AND PUMPKIN MINI QUICHES

Cook quiches the morning of party, reheat just before serving.

3 sheets ready rolled puff pastry
2 bacon rashers, finely chopped
1 onion, finely chopped
⅔ cup mashed pumpkin
1 cup grated smoked cheese
1 egg, lightly beaten
¼ cup milk
pinch nutmeg
1 bacon rasher, extra
Cut pastry into 7cm circles with a fluted cutter, press into shallow patty pans. Cook bacon and onion in frying pan until bacon is crisp, drain. Stir bacon mixture into combined pumpkin, cheese, egg, milk and nutmeg, spoon into pastry cases. Cut extra bacon into thin strips, roll up, place a piece on each quiche. Bake in hot oven 15 minutes, reduce heat to moderate, bake 10 minutes or until golden brown, serve hot.

Makes 24.

CHICKEN AND LEEK PIE

Chicken mixture (without potatoes on top) can be cooked ahead, cooled and frozen for up to 1 month. Thaw in refrigerator 24 hours before the party. Top with potatoes and cheese several hours before re-heating, cover, reheat 30 minutes in moderate oven, uncover, continue to bake until browned.

4 bacon rashers, chopped
15g butter
3 leeks, finely sliced
6 zucchini, sliced
2 tablespoons oil
16 chicken thigh fillets, chopped
1kg potatoes, sliced
15g butter, extra
½ cup grated tasty cheese
CHEESE SAUCE
45g butter
1 clove garlic, crushed
1 chicken stock cube, crumbled
¼ cup plain flour
2 cups milk
1 cup grated tasty cheese
¼ cup grated parmesan cheese
Cook bacon in frying pan until crisp. Add butter, leeks and zucchini, cook 5 minutes or until leeks are tender. Remove from pan.

Heat oil in the pan, add chicken gradually, cook over high heat until lightly browned all over, all to bacon mixture with cheese sauce, mix well. Place in shallow ovenproof dish, top with potatoes. Brush with extra melted butter, sprinkle with cheese, bake in moderately hot oven 60 minutes or until golden brown.

Cheese Sauce: Melt butter in saucepan, add garlic, stock cube and flour, cook 1 minute, stirring. Gradually stir in milk, stir until sauce boils and thickens, add cheeses, stir until melted.

LAMB IN RED WINE SAUCE

The most important part of this recipe is the browning of the lamb so follow recipe carefully. To freeze this dish, omit onions, garlic, mushrooms and carrots. Cook the lamb in the oil until brown, proceed as directed below, cool, remove bay leaves, freeze for up to a month. Thaw in refrigerator 24 hours before the party. Cook onions, garlic and mushrooms as directed below, add to lamb mixture with carrots; cover, heat until carrots are tender. This can be done up to several hours before serving. This recipe is not suitable to microwave.

2 large legs of lamb, boned
2 tablespoons oil
24 baby onions
2 cloves garlic, crushed
500g baby mushrooms
⅓ cup plain flour
2 cups dry red wine
420g can beef consomme
1 cup water
¼ cup tomato paste
½ cup red currant jelly
2 bay leaves
½ teaspoon dried thyme leaves
4 carrots, chopped

2 tablespoons chopped parsley
Trim lamb, cut into bite-sized pieces. Heat oil in large frying pan, add whole onions and garlic, cook, stirring, until onions are lightly browned, remove from pan. Add lamb gradually to pan in single layer, cook, stirring constantly, over high heat until the meat is well browned all over. This might have to be done in several batches depending on the size of the pan. Add the mushrooms and onion mixture to pan and sprinkle with flour. Stir in wine, undiluted consomme, water, tomato paste, jelly, bay leaves and thyme. Bring to the boil, reduce heat and simmer uncovered for 1 hour, stirring occasionally. Add carrots, cook 15 minutes, or until tender. Remove and discard bay leaves, sprinkle with parsley.

STIR-FRIED VEGETABLES WITH ALMONDS

Broccoli and carrots can be cooked up to 12 hours ahead, covered with chilled water and refrigerated. Almonds can be fried, drained and stored in an airtight container for up to a week before required. This recipe tastes and looks best if served immediately. This recipe is not suitable to freeze.

750g broccoli
6 carrots, thinly sliced
2 tablespoons oil
155g (1 cup) blanched almonds
2 teaspoons grated fresh ginger
2 cloves garlic, crushed
1 red pepper, sliced
3 teaspoons oyster sauce
3 teaspoons dark soya sauce
1 teaspoon sesame oil
2½ tablespoons cornflour
2 cups water
1 chicken stock cube, crumbled
4 green shallots, chopped
Cut broccoli into small flowerets and boil, steam or microwave with carrots until they are just tender. Drain, then rinse under cold water, drain and pat dry with absorbent paper.

Heat oil in a wok or large frying pan, add almonds and cook, stirring over high heat until they are golden brown. Remove almonds from pan, drain on absorbent paper.

Add ginger, garlic and pepper to pan, stir-fry 1 minute, add oyster sauce, soya sauce, sesame oil and vegetables, stir-fry 1 minute. Blend cornflour with a little of the water, add to pan or wok with remaining water and stock cube, stir constantly, over high heat until mixture boils and thickens. Stir in almonds and shallots; serve immediately with boiled rice or fruity brown rice.

FRUITY BROWN RICE

The rice can be cooked a month before required and frozen. Combine thawed rice with raisin mixture the day before the party and store the mixture covered in refrigerator. This recipe is not suitable to microwave.

3 cups brown rice
130g (¾ cup) chopped raisins
2 teaspoons dark rum
2 teaspoons dark soya sauce
1½ tablespoons oil
¼ teaspoon ground cinnamon
2 teaspoons grated orange rind
2 tablespoons orange juice
1 tablespoon lemon juice
1 tablespoon honey
1 red pepper, chopped
1 green pepper, chopped
¼ cup chopped parsley

Cook rice in large saucepan of boiling water for 30 minutes, drain. Combine raisins, rum, soya sauce, oil, cinnamon, orange rind, juices and honey, stand while rice is cooking.

Combine rice, add the raisin mixture to serving bowl, stir in peppers and parsley. Refrigerate covered, until serving time.

HAM AND CHUTNEY BREADSTICKS

Breadsticks can be prepared, wrapped in foil and frozen for up to a month. Bake, while still frozen, for about 20 minutes in a moderate oven. This recipe is not suitable to microwave.

3 medium breadsticks
185g butter, softened
3 tablespoons apricot chutney
1 teaspoon lemon juice
2 tablespoons chopped parsley
2 cloves garlic, peeled
4 slices ham

Cut bread diagonally into thick slices, do not cut right through. Process butter, chutney, lemon juice, parsley, garlic and ham until smooth. Spread butter mixture onto one side of each slice. Wrap breadsticks in foil, bake in moderate oven for 10 minutes.

CHOCOLATE RUM SPONGE

Make and assemble the cake a day ahead. Decorate with whipped cream, almonds and strawberries before serving. This recipe is not suitable to freeze or microwave.

200g dark chocolate, chopped
2 packets sponge mix
½ cup castor sugar
½ cup water

½ cup dark rum
FILLING
400g ricotta cheese
2 tablespoons dark rum
300g carton sour cream
2 teaspoons grated orange rind
100g dark chocolate
TOPPING
½ cup flaked almonds
2 x 300ml cartons thickened cream
250g punnet strawberries

Melt chocolate over hot water, cool to lukewarm. Make sponges according to packet directions; beat in chocolate.

Pour into greased and lined deep 25cm round cake pan. Bake in moderate oven for about 45 minutes, stand 5 minutes, before turning onto wire rack to cool.

Split cold cake into 4 layers. Combine sugar and water in saucepan, stir constantly over heat, without boiling, until sugar is dissolved, bring to the boil, boil 3 minutes without stirring, remove from heat, stir in rum. Brush each layer of cake with rum syrup, layer cake with filling. Decorate with topping several hours before serving.

Filling: Beat the ricotta cheese, rum, sour cream and orange rind together in small bowl with electric mixer until smooth. Grate 30g of the chocolate, chop and melt remaining chocolate over hot water, cool to lukewarm. Beat the melted chocolate into the cheese mixture, stir in the grated chocolate.

Topping: Toast almonds on oven tray in moderate oven for 5 minutes, cool. Whip cream until soft peaks form and spread all over cake. Press almonds onto side of cake and decorate with halved strawberries.

FROZEN MANGO MOUSSE

Make up to 3 days ahead.

½ cup sugar
½ cup water
8 eggs, separated
2 teaspoons grated orange rind
6 ripe mangoes
1⅓ cups sugar, extra
⅔ cup water, extra
2 x 300ml cartons thickened cream

Combine sugar and water in saucepan, stir constantly over heat, without boiling, until sugar is dissolved. Bring to the boil, boil 3 minutes without stirring, or until thick and syrupy.

Beat the egg yolks and orange rind in a small bowl with electric mixer until it becomes thick, pour in hot sugar syrup in a thin stream while motor is operating. Continue beating the mixture for about 5 minutes or until it becomes very thick. Transfer mixture to large bowl.

Blend or process mango pulp until it is smooth and beat it into egg yolk mixture. Continue beating this mixture for a further 5 minutes.

Combine extra sugar and extra water in saucepan, stir constantly over heat, without boiling, until sugar is dissolved. Bring to the boil, boil rapidly, without stirring, until a small amount of syrup dropped in cold water forms a hard ball. If using a candy thermometer boil until syrup reaches 120°C (248°F).

While sugar syrup is cooking, beat egg whites on high speed in large bowl with electric mixer until firm peaks form; while motor is operating, gradually pour in hot syrup in thin steady stream. Gently stir in mango and egg yolk mixture. Beat cream until soft peaks form, fold gently into mango mixture. Pour mixture evenly into 2 moulds (6 cup capacity each), cover tightly with foil, freeze several hours or overnight until firm.

LEMON CHOCOLATE SQUARES

These squares can be made 2 days ahead and kept covered in the refrigerator. Slice can be frozen for up to a month. This recipe is not suitable to microwave.

185g butter, chopped
100g dark chocolate, chopped
1 egg, lightly beaten
250g packet plain chocolate
 biscuits, finely crushed
1 cup coconut
80g (⅔ cup) finely chopped pecans
 or walnuts
FILLING
90g butter
2 cups icing sugar
2 tablespoons lemon juice
yellow food colouring
TOPPING
50g dark chocolate, chopped
2 teaspoons butter

Melt butter and chocolate in double saucepan or heatproof bowl over hot water. Remove from heat and stir in egg, biscuits, coconut and nuts.

Press mixture firmly but evenly over the base of a lightly greased 19cm x 29cm lamington pan. Spread filling evenly over the base, drizzle with topping. Refrigerate for several hours before cutting.

Filling: Cream butter with sifted icing sugar and lemon juice in small bowl with electric mixer until it becomes light and fluffy. Tint yellow with colouring to desired colour.

Topping: Melt chocolate and butter in double saucepan or heatproof bowl over hot water and cool to lukewarm before using.

SPECIAL OCCASIONS

6 NEW YEAR'S PARTY FOR 10

Main course salads are excellent to serve to a large or small crowd. Each of these salads, as an individual meal, will serve 4 people. Serve all of these salads if your guests are hearty eaters or select only 3 salads.

CREAMY EGG MOUSSE

Mousse can be made a day ahead, keep covered in refrigerator. Serve with toast, Melba toast or crackers. This recipe is not suitable to freeze.

6 hard-boiled eggs, chopped
¾ cup mayonnaise
3 teaspoons gelatine
¾ cup water
1 chicken stock cube, crumbled
½ cup thickened cream
1 tablespoon anchovy sauce
few drops tabasco

Combine eggs and mayonnaise in bowl. Sprinkle gelatine over water, dissolve over hot water, mix in stock cube. Stir gelatine mixture into egg mixture, fold in whipped cream and sauces. Pour into lightly oiled round 20cm cake pan, refrigerate until set.
To unmould mousse: Dip base of pan into hot water for a second or two, turn onto serving plate. Garnish with tomato, olives and watercress if desired.

CURRIED SCALLOP-STUFFED MUSHROOMS

Prepare mushrooms as close to serving time as possible. This recipe is not suitable to freeze or microwave.

20 small mushrooms
oil
½ cup water
½ cup dry white wine
250g scallops
30g butter
1 teaspoon curry powder
1 clove garlic, crushed
4 green shallots, chopped
¼ cup chopped parsley
2 teaspoons lemon juice
1½ cups stale breadcrumbs
1 tablespoon mayonnaise
2 bacon rashers, chopped
60g butter, melted, extra

Choose flat even-sized mushrooms; remove stems, place mushrooms on oven tray, brush lightly with oil.

Combine water and wine in saucepan, bring to the boil, add scallops, remove from heat, stand 2 minutes; drain, chop when cool.

Melt butter in saucepan, add curry powder, garlic and shallots. Cook, stirring, few minutes. Stir in parsley, lemon juice, breadcrumbs and mayonnaise. Cook bacon in frying pan until crisp, drain, add to breadcrumb mixture with half the extra butter and scallops.

Place spoonfuls of mixture into mushroom caps, drizzle with remaining extra butter, bake in moderate oven for about 10 minutes.

CHICKEN LIVER SALAD

Salad is best prepared as close to serving time as possible.

1kg chicken livers
1 cup dry white wine
1 teaspoon grated fresh ginger
1 clove garlic, crushed
30g butter, melted
1 lettuce
1 green pepper, sliced
125g mushrooms, sliced
DRESSING
3 bacon rashers, chopped
1 small onion, finely chopped
¼ cup oil
2 tablespoons white vinegar
¼ teaspoon dried oregano leaves
¼ teaspoon dried basil leaves
60g black olives, halved

Place cleaned livers in bowl with wine, ginger and garlic, stand 2 hours. Pat livers dry with absorbent paper, place on griller tray, brush with butter. Grill a few minutes on each side, or until tender. Cut livers in half when cool.

Line salad bowl with lettuce, add pepper and mushrooms to bowl, add livers, then dressing, toss lightly.
Dressing: Cook bacon and onion in frying pan until bacon is crisp; drain on absorbent paper. Combine oil, vinegar, oregano, basil, bacon mixture and olives in bowl, mix well.

HEARTS OF PALM SALAD WITH TARRAGON DRESSING

Prepare as close to serving time as possible, for best results.

1 lettuce
8 green shallots, chopped
1 avocado, sliced
250g cooked prawns, shelled
400g can hearts of palm, drained, chopped
190g can pimientos, drained, sliced
TARRAGON DRESSING
⅓ cup oil
2 tablespoons tarragon vinegar
1 teaspoon French mustard

Tear lettuce into large pieces, place in salad bowl with shallots, avocado, prawns, hearts of palm and pimientos. Add dressing, toss lightly.

6 NEW YEAR PARTY FOR 10

Creamy Egg Mousse

Curried Scallop-Stuffed Mushrooms

Chicken Liver Salad

Hearts of Palm Salad with Tarragon Dressing

Quail Salad with Walnut Dressing

Scallop and Endive Salad with Lemon Dressing

Chinese Duck Salad

Mocha Almond Ice-Cream Bombe

Mango Marnier Mousse Cake

Tarragon Dressing: Combine oil, vinegar and mustard in bowl; mix well.

QUAIL SALAD WITH WALNUT DRESSING

Quail can be cooked a day ahead. Prepare salad just before serving.

30g butter
¼ cup oil
6 quail
2 mignonette lettuce
8 green shallots, chopped
1 onion, finely sliced
1 red pepper, chopped
60g mushrooms, sliced

WALNUT DRESSING
⅓ **cup oil**
2 tablespoons white vinegar
1 tablespoon sour cream
2 tablespoons chopped parsley
¼ **cup chopped walnuts**
Heat butter and oil in baking dish on top of stove, add quail, brush with oil mixture. Bake uncovered in moderate oven, for about 30 minutes, turning once during cooking time. When quail are cold, cut into quarters. Tear lettuce into large pieces, place lettuce in salad bowl with shallots, onion, pepper and mushrooms. Add quail and dressing; toss lightly.

Walnut Dressing: Combine oil, vinegar, sour cream, parsley and walnuts in bowl, mix well.

SCALLOP AND ENDIVE SALAD WITH LEMON DRESSING

Prepare close to serving time.

1kg scallops
1 bunch endive
1 red pepper, sliced
2 teaspoons drained canned green peppercorns
LEMON DRESSING
1 teaspoon grated lemon rind

Left: Creamy Egg Mousse; right: Curried Scallop-Stuffed Mushrooms

¼ **cup lemon juice**
1 teaspoon grated fresh ginger
2 tablespoons oil
Bring large shallow frying pan of water to the boil, add scallops, remove from heat, cover, stand 2 minutes; drain well. Tear green tips from endive, place in salad bowl with pepper, peppercorns and scallops, toss with dressing.
Lemon Dressing: Combine all ingredients; mix well.

SPECIAL OCCASIONS

CHINESE DUCK SALAD

Ducks can be baked up to 2 days ahead or roast ducks can be bought from stores which stock fresh Asian foods. Prepare salad as close to serving time as possible. Ducks are not suitable to microwave.

2 x No. 15 ducks
30g butter
1 carrot
1 cucumber
¼ cup sugar
¼ cup water
1 red pepper
3 sticks celery
MUSTARD DRESSING
1½ teaspoons French mustard
1½ teaspoons English mustard
¼ cup lemon juice
¼ cup oil
½ teaspoon sugar

Place ducks on rack in large baking dish, rub well with butter. Bake in moderately hot oven for about 1 hour or until ducks are golden brown and tender. Baste ducks with pan juices every 15 minutes during cooking. Cool ducks to room temperature. Remove bones from ducks; discard bones. Cut duck flesh into 1cm strips.

Cut carrot into thin strips. Cut cucumber in half lengthways, remove seeds, cut into strips.

Combine sugar and water in small saucepan, stir constantly over heat, without boiling, until sugar is dissolved, boil 1 minute without stirring. Stand a few minutes, add carrot and cucumber, stand 30 minutes, drain.

Cut pepper and celery, into strips. Combine duck and vegetables in salad bowl with dressing; toss lightly.

Mustard Dressing: Combine all ingredients; mix well.

MOCHA ALMOND ICE-CREAM BOMBE

Bombe can be made up to a week ahead; keep covered with foil in freezer. Kahlua and Tia Maria are coffee-flavoured liqueurs while Amaretto is almond-flavoured.

8 eggs, separated
2 cups icing sugar
2 x 300ml cartons thickened cream
1 tablespoon dry instant coffee
1 tablespoon Kahlua or Tia Maria
¼ cup flaked almonds
1 tablespoon Amaretto
125g dark chocolate
250g dark chocolate, extra
30g Copha

Beat egg whites in large bowl with electric mixer until soft peaks form, gradually add sifted icing sugar, beat

Clockwise from back top: Scallop and Endive Salad with Lemon Dressing; Chicken Liver Salad; Chinese Duck Salad; Hearts of Palm Salad with Tarragon Dressing; Quail Salad with Walnut Dressing

until sugar is dissolved. Beat cream in large bowl until firm. Fold cream gently through egg white mixture, divide mixture evenly into 3 bowls. Beat egg yolks lightly with fork, divide egg yolks evenly into 3 cups.

Add coffee powder and Kahlua to 1 cup containing egg yolks, fold evenly through 1 bowl of the egg white mixture, pour into 10 cup pudding steamer, level top, cover with foil, freeze for about 30 minutes or until ice-cream feels firm. Place remaining bowls of egg white mixture into refrigerator while waiting for each layer of ice-cream to set.

Toast almonds in moderate oven on oven tray for 5 minutes, cool. Add Amaretto to another cup containing egg yolks, fold into another bowl of egg white mixture with almonds, spread evenly over coffee ice-cream, cover, freeze 30 minutes or until firm.

Melt chocolate over hot water, cool, stir into remaining egg yolks, fold into remaining egg white mixture, spread evenly over almond ice-cream, cover, freeze overnight. Invert ice-cream onto

serving plate, return to freezer while melting extra chocolate.

Melt extra chocolate over hot water, remove from heat, add Copha, stir until melted, pour as evenly as possible over ice-cream, return to freezer.

MANGO MARNIER MOUSSE CAKE

Grand Marnier is an orange-flavoured liqueur. Cake can be assembled a day ahead. Decorate about 6 hours before serving. This recipe is not suitable to freeze or microwave.

1 packet sponge mix
¼ cup orange juice
2 tablespoons Grand Marnier
2 x 300ml cartons thickened cream
FILLING
3 ripe mangoes, chopped
2 tablespoons sugar
3 tablespoons Grand Marnier
3 teaspoons gelatine
3 tablespoons orange juice
300ml carton thickened cream

Make cake as directed on packet. Pour mixture into greased deep 23cm round

Left: Mocha Almond Ice-Cream Bombe; right: Mango Marnier Mousse Cake

cake pan, bake in moderate oven for about 40 minutes. Turn onto wire rack to cool.

Cut cake into 4 layers. Place a layer on a serving plate, brush with combined orange juice and Grand Marnier. Spread with one-third of the filling; repeat layering. Cover cake, refrigerate 1 hour or until set. Spread top and side of cake with whipped cream. Then decorate with mango slices and kiwi fruit, if desired.

Filling: Blend or process mangoes and sugar until smooth. Push purée through a sieve, you will need 1 cup of purée for this recipe. Stir Grand Marnier into mango purée. Sprinkle gelatine over orange juice, dissolve over hot water. Add gelatine to mango mixture, fold in whipped cream, refrigerate until mixture is almost set, stirring every few minutes so that the outside does not set before the centre. Stir mixture until smooth just before spreading on the cake.

Clockwise from back: Strawberry Champagne Punch; Pineapple and Vermouth Punch; Citrus Honey Punch; Orange Mango Cointreau Punch; Coconut Pineapple Mint Punch

PUNCHES

Put a little punch into any occasion with our cool thirst-quenchers made for summer entertaining. Punches with and without alcohol are included. Make sure all ingredients are well chilled before mixing them together; always add aerated drinks just before serving. Add ice to individual glasses to stop diluting the punch.

ORANGE MANGO COINTREAU PUNCH

Cointreau is a citrus-flavoured liqueur.

2 cups orange juice
1 cup canned coconut cream
2 tablespoons icing sugar
⅓ cup Cointreau
2 tablespoons brandy
2 x 425g cans mangoes, drained

Combine orange juice, coconut cream, sifted icing sugar, liqueur and brandy in serving bowl; mix well. Blend or process three-quarters of the mangoes until smooth, stir into orange mixture. Chop remaining mangoes into cubes, add to punch, refrigerate.

Makes about 1½ litres (6 cups).

CITRUS HONEY PUNCH

1 cup orange juice
2 tablespoons lemon juice
1 cup grapefruit juice
1 tablespoon honey
1 cup canned pineapple juice
1 tablespoon passionfruit cordial
1 cup lemonade

Combine orange juice, lemon juice, grapefruit juice, honey, pineapple juice and cordial in serving bowl; mix well. Add lemonade just before serving.

Makes about 1¼ litres (5 cups).

STRAWBERRY CHAMPAGNE PUNCH

Grand Marnier and Cointreau are citrus-flavoured liqueurs.

3 x 250g punnets strawberries
⅔ cup icing sugar
⅓ cup Grand Marnier or Cointreau
2 tablespoons lemon juice
2 x 750ml bottles champagne

Chop half a punnet of strawberries; reserve for decorating.

Blend or process remaining strawberries with icing sugar, liqueur and lemon juice until smooth, place into serving bowl. Add champagne and reserved chopped strawberries just before serving.

Makes about 2½ litres (10 cups).

COCONUT PINEAPPLE MINT PUNCH

Creme de Menthe is a mint liqueur.

420g can coconut cream
½ cup vodka
3 cups canned sweetened pineapple juice
1 tablespoon icing sugar
1½ tablespoons Crème de Menthe

Combine coconut cream, vodka, pineapple juice, sifted icing sugar and liqueur in serving bowl; mix well. Refrigerate before serving.

Makes about 1½ litres (6 cups).

PINEAPPLE AND VERMOUTH PUNCH

Crème de Menthe is a mint liqueur.

3 cups canned sweetened pineapple juice
2 tablespoons Crème de Menthe
⅓ cup dry vermouth
2 tablespoons icing sugar
2 cups lemonade

Combine pineapple juice, liqueur, vermouth and sifted icing sugar in serving bowl; mix well. Add lemonade just before serving.

Makes about 1½ litres (6 cups).

APRICOT PINEAPPLE PUNCH

850ml can apricot nectar
850ml can unsweetened pineapple juice
3 passionfruit
2 oranges, sliced
2 cups soda water

Combine apricot nectar, pineapple juice, passionfruit pulp and oranges in serving bowl; refrigerate. Add soda water just before serving.

Makes about 2¼ litres (9 cups).

FRUIT SHERRY PUNCH

1 cup orange juice
1 cup apple juice
¾ cup dry sherry
1 lemon, sliced
½ cucumber, sliced
2 cups ginger ale
2 cups soda water

Combine orange juice, apple juice, sherry, lemon and cucumber in serving bowl; mix well, refrigerate. Add ginger ale and soda water just before serving.

Makes about 1¾ litres (7 cups).

CHERRY ROSE PUNCH

½ cup sugar
½ cup water
750ml bottle rosé wine
2 tablespoons lemon juice
1 apple, peeled
250g black cherries, pitted
2 cups soda water

Combine sugar and water in saucepan, stir constantly over heat without boiling until sugar is dissolved. Bring to the boil, boil 1 minute, remove from heat, cool.

From left: Cherry Rosé Punch; Fruit Sherry Punch; Apricot Pineapple Punch; Fresh Pineapple Tea Punch

Combine rosé wine with lemon juice and sugar syrup in serving bowl; refrigerate. Process apple and cherries until chopped, add to bowl with soda water just before serving.

Makes about 1½ litres (6 cups).

FRESH PINEAPPLE TEA PUNCH

After making tea, allow it to cool to room temperature without refrigerating before using.

1 ripe pineapple, peeled
2 cups cold black tea, strained
2 tablespoons lemon juice
2 x 285ml bottles dry ginger ale

Remove core from pineapple, chop pineapple roughly. Blend or process pineapple and tea until pineapple is finely crushed. Refrigerate until cold. Add lemon juice and ginger ale just before serving.

Makes about 1½ litres (6 cups).

Traditional ◆ Christmas

FAVOURITES

We have gathered our most requested cake and pudding recipes in this section and combined them with information on the finer points of making these delights. The results are rich and festive and suitable not only for Christmas but for a range of occasions.

Table: Appley Hoare Antiques; china: Lifestyle Imports "Taitu"

Clockwise from top: Grand Marnier Fruit Cake; Irish Fruit Cake; The Australian Women's Weekly Fruit Cake.

THE AUSTRALIAN WOMEN'S WEEKLY FRUIT CAKE

This cake is our traditional stand-by; it keeps and cuts well. The recipe does not include self-raising flour or any other raising agent.

500g (3¼ cups) sultanas
250g (1½ cups) raisins, chopped
125g (¾ cup) currants
125g (½ cup) mixed peel
125g (⅔ cup) glacé cherries, quartered
2 tablespoons marmalade
½ cup rum
250g butter
1 teaspoon grated orange rind
1 teaspoon grated lemon rind
1 cup brown sugar, firmly packed
4 eggs
2 cups plain flour
2 teaspoons mixed spice

Combine all fruit, marmalade and rum in large bowl; mix well. Cream butter and rinds in small bowl with electric mixer until just smooth, add sugar, beat until just combined. Add eggs one at a time, beat only until ingredients are combined between additions. Add creamed mixture to fruit mixture, mix well. Mix in the sifted dry ingredients thoroughly.

Spread mixture into a deep 19cm square or a deep 23cm round prepared cake pan. Bake in a slow oven for 3 to 3½ hours.

GRAND MARNIER FRUIT CAKE

500g (3¼ cups) sultanas
250g (1 cup) mixed peel
125g (¾ cup) chopped raisins
125g (¾ cup) chopped dates
125g (½ cup) chopped dried plums (prunes)
125g (½ cup) chopped glacé apricots
125g (½ cup) chopped glacé pineapple
60g (½ cup) slivered almonds
½ cup pecans or walnuts
1 tablespoon grated orange rind
½ cup castor sugar
¼ cup orange juice
½ cup Grand Marnier
250g butter
½ cup brown sugar
5 eggs
2 cups plain flour

Combine fruits, nuts and rind in large bowl; mix well. Sprinkle castor sugar evenly into heavy-based frying pan, place over medium heat, cook until sugar begins to melt and brown, gently stir until completely melted and golden brown. Remove from heat, add orange juice, return to heat, stir constantly until toffee pieces are dissolved. Do not boil as this will evaporate too much of the liquid. Add Grand Marnier, strain liquid to remove any small pieces of toffee; cool to room temperature.

Place fruit mixture in airtight container or large jar with tight-fitting screw-top, pour Grand Marnier mixture over fruit mixture. Seal, stand overnight. Next day, invert jar or mix fruit mixture well. Do this for 10 days (up to a month is fine).

Beat butter until soft, add brown sugar, beat until combined. Add eggs one at a time, beat until combined before adding next egg. Pour fruit mixture into large bowl, add creamed mixture, mix well. Add sifted flour, mix well. Spread mixture into deep 19cm square or deep 23cm round prepared cake pan. Bake in slow oven for 3 to 3½ hours.

To decorate cake with marzipan oranges: Use a packet of almond paste. Dust hands with pure icing sugar. Roll pieces of paste into balls, place small part of clove on orange. Use skewer to roll orange over a grater to give effect of skin. Stand oranges on wire rack to dry overnight. Paint with orange food colouring.

IRISH FRUIT CAKE

375g (2¼ cups) raisins, chopped
375g (2¼ cups) sultanas
90g (½ cup) glacé cherries, quartered
90g (⅔ cup) chopped dates
¼ cup chopped dried plums (prunes)
¼ cup chopped glacé pineapple
¼ cup mixed peel
1 teaspoon grated lemon rind
1 teaspoon grated orange rind
2 tablespoons lemon juice
¼ cup orange juice
⅓ cup whisky
1 small apple, peeled, grated
185g butter
¾ cup castor sugar
3 eggs
¼ cup chopped pecans or walnuts
¼ cup ground almonds
1½ cups plain flour
¼ teaspoon ground nutmeg
½ teaspoon ground cinnamon

Combine fruit in large bowl with rinds, juices, whisky and apple; cover, stand up to 3 weeks in cool dark place. Stir mixture every few days.

Cream butter and sugar in small bowl with electric mixer until combined, add eggs one at a time, beating until combined between each addition. Add to fruit mixture with nuts and sifted dry ingredients, mix well. Spread mixture into deep 19cm square or

THE FINER POINTS OF MAKING FRUIT CAKES

The size of a fruit cake is determined by the amount of butter used in the recipe, for example, a 250g cake mixture (previously known as a ½lb mixture) contains 250g butter and will make a deep 23cm round or a deep 19cm square cake. Cake bought from cake shops are, however, sold by the weight of the cake after it has been cooked.

Before making a rich fruit cake, prepare cake pans and check that the oven shelf is in correct position.

Cake pan sizes: If using cake pans of an unusual shape (oval, hexagonal or similar), there is a simple way to determine how much mixture each pan will require. Fill a deep 19cm square or deep 23cm round cake pan with water, pour this water into the shaped pan. Each pan full of water will represent a 250g fruit cake mixture.

Preparing the oven: As a guide, the top of the cooked cake should be in the centre of the oven; arrange the shelves accordingly. If baking more than one fruit cake at a time, check that they will fit by arranging the empty cake pans in the oven. It is important to allow even circulation of heat. The pans must not touch each other, or the sides or back of the oven, or the door when it is closed. Most ovens are not large enough to take more than one shelf of fruit cakes at a time, but if the oven is adequate and there is room for heat circulation around all the pans, the results will be good. The positions of the cakes must be changed halfway during the cooking time — move the lower cakes to the top shelf of the oven and vice versa.

When cooking more than one cake on a shelf, best results will be obtained if their positions are changed about halfway through the cooking time as many ovens brown unevenly. Opening the oven door for a short period will not affect the cakes in any way. When cooking more than one cake at a time, the total cooking time will be a little longer, due to more absorption of heat.

It is important that the oven shelves be level, particularly if the cake is to be decorated as an uneven cake will need wasteful trimming. This can be checked with a spirit level or a shallow tray of water. Most stoves have small adjusting legs underneath to counteract uneven kitchen floors.

Lining cake pans: To ensure a well-shaped cake, cake pans must be lined correctly. Lining paper protects the cake during the long cooking time, the longer the cooking time, the heavier the lining paper needs to be. If pans are larger than 23cm in diameter, use 1 thickness of brown paper and 3 to 4 thicknesses of greaseproof or baking paper. For smaller cakes, use 3 to 4 thicknesses of greaseproof or baking paper on base and sides.

For baking times of more than 3 hours, the lining paper should stand up around the edge of the pan (by about 5 cm) to protect the top of the cake. The following method of lining a round or square cake pan allows for this.

For sides, cut long strips of paper, 10cm wider than the depth of the pan. Fold each strip lengthways about 2cm from edge and make diagonal cuts up to the fold, about 2cm apart. This enables the paper to fit readily around the curves or corners of the pan, with cut section in base. Use base of pan as cutting guide for paper to line base; put base paper in position **(below)**.

There is another method of insula-

ting the cake mixture from the heat during the long cooking time. Grease the cake pan evenly, dust with flour, shake out excess flour. Cover base of pan with piece of greaseproof or baking paper. Fold 3 large opened-out sheets of newspaper lengthways into 4. Wrap the paper around the outside of the cake pan, secure the paper with string. Place a thick folded piece of newspaper onto an oven tray, stand the cake on the paper before baking

the cake. This is a particularly good method when an even-shaped cake is required for cake decorating **(below)**.

Mixing the cake: It is important to have the eggs and butter at room temperature. Beat butter with electric mixer, wooden spoon, or by hand until it just clings to the side of the bowl, do not beat until pale in colour. Add sugar (sift sugar if it is lumpy), beat only until combined (over-creaming of butter or butter/sugar at this stage could result in a crumbly cake). Add eggs one at a time, beat only until each egg has been absorbed by the butter mixture. There is less chance of curdling the mixture if the eggs are added fairly quickly.

Add fruit mixture to creamed mixture, mix ingredients well together with hand; a wooden spoon will not break up any clumps of fruit. Mix in sifted flour and spice. Place into prepared cake pan, drop pan from a height of about 15cm to break any large air bubbles and settle mixture in pan, bake as directed. Level top of cake mixture with spatula. If top of cake is to be decorated with cherries and almonds press gently onto top of cake mixture before baking **(below)**.

Note: Most rich fruit cakes do not contain any raising agent. If desired, a rich fruit cake mixture can be prepared ahead, placed in the prepared pan, the surface of the mixture covered with greaseproof or baking paper or plastic wrap, and the pan placed in refrigerator for up to 1 week. Allow cake to stand 6 hours or overnight to return to room temperature before baking. If taken straight from the refrigerator to the oven, a cold cake will take about 30 minutes longer to cook than if it is allowed to return to room temperature. Refrigerator storage is a help when making several cakes, particularly for tiered cakes.

Cooking time: If in doubt about the accuracy of your oven, have the temperature checked professionally (usually through your local council or stove's manufacturer), or buy an oven thermometer (from a hardware store) and leave it in the oven during cooking so you can check the temperature while the cake is cooking.

To test if cake is cooked: After minimum specified cooking time, feel top of cake with fingertips. If cake feels firm, use the blade of a sharp pointed vegetable knife to test cake. Gently push the knife into the thickest part of the cake, right through to the base of the cake pan. Gently withdraw the knife and feel the blade; if the blade is simply sticky from fruit, the cake is cooked, but if there is moist cake mixture on the blade, return the cake to the oven for a further 15 minutes before testing again.

When cake is cooked: Remove from oven, tear away lining paper from around top of pan or remove newspaper collar; leave cake still in its pan. Brush cake evenly with about 2 tablespoons of extra whisky, rum, brandy or sherry, cover top lightly with foil. This is to trap steam and give a softer top surface to cake. Wrap cake, still in its pan, in a clean towel, and leave until cold (up to 24 hours).

If cake is to be decorated a good flat top is required. The top becomes the bottom for decorated cakes, so turn the hot, foil-covered cake, still in its pan, upside down on a flat surface; the cake's own weight will flatten the top surface and minimise trimming.

To store: When cake is cold, remove it from the pan, leave lining paper intact, wrap tightly in plastic wrap, then in foil or a towel; store in a cool place. Rich fruit cakes can be stored in the refrigerator for at least a year. Cakes can be frozen if desired.

FAVOURITES

Prize Winning Fruit Cake

THREE-IN-ONE MIX

The basic fruit mixture given below is for people who want to be well organised for the busy festive time. The mixture can be prepared at least a month before you are ready to use it, however, it will keep indefinitely if covered, to exclude the air. Simply stir the ingredients occasionally. Store in a cool dark place; the refrigerator is ideal.

We used Grand Marnier in this recipe to tie in with the citrus flavour, but sherry, rum, brandy or whisky can be used instead, if preferred. We used Granny Smith apples in this recipe.

The cake, pudding and tarts can all be frozen for at least 3 months, but there is really no advantage in this.

This fruit mixture recipe is not suitable to microwave.

BASIC FRUIT MIXTURE

1kg (6½ cups) sultanas
375g (2¼ cups) currants
375g (2¼ cups) raisins, chopped
250g (1½ cups) chopped dates
250g (1½ cups) chopped dried
  plums (prunes)
250g (1½ cups) glacé cherries,
  quartered
125g (½ cup) chopped glacé
  apricots
125g (½ cup) chopped glacé
  pineapple
125g (½ cup) chopped glacé ginger
125g (½ cup) mixed peel
3 apples, peeled, grated
250g jar (⅔ cup) fig jam
2 tablespoons grated orange rind
½ cup orange juice
1 tablespoon grated lemon rind
¼ cup lemon juice
2 cups (500g) brown sugar
1 tablespoon mixed spice
1⅓ cups Grand Marnier

Combine all ingredients in large bowl, mix well with hand to combine ingredients thoroughly. Cover tightly with plastic wrap to exclude air. Place in cool dark cupboard for at least a month before using.

MOIST CHRISTMAS CAKE

250g butter, melted, cooled
5 eggs, lightly beaten
2½ cups plain flour
half the Basic Fruit Mixture

Place half of the Basic Fruit Mixture into large bowl (the remaining half is used for the pudding and tarts). Use your hand to mix in half the butter, eggs and sifted flour, then remaining butter, eggs and flour. Mix thoroughly to break up any lumps of fruit which are clinging together.

Spread evenly into deep 19cm

deep 23cm round prepared cake pan. Bake in a slow oven for 3 to 3½ hours.

PRIZE WINNING FRUIT CAKE

This recipe won £100 in an Australian Women's Weekly cookery competition in 1937. Throughout the years we have had countless requests for the recipe so we have included it in this section.

We have converted the imperial measurements to metric measurements but the quantity remains the same. The recipe can be halved if preferred and cooked in either a deep 19cm square or deep 23cm round prepared cake pan. The cooking time for the smaller cakes will be about 3 hours in a slow oven.

500g (3¼ cups) sultanas
500g (3¼ cups) currants
250g (1½ cups) chopped raisins
125g (⅔ cup) glacé cherries, halved
⅓ cup mixed peel
185g (1½ cups) blanched almonds,
  halved
⅓ cup orange marmalade
1 tablespoon grated orange rind
2 teaspoons grated lemon rind
¼ cup lemon juice
⅔ cup brandy
500g butter
500g (2 cups) brown sugar, firmly
  packed
8 eggs
3 cups plain flour
1 cup self-raising flour

Combine fruit, almonds, marmalade, rinds, juice and brandy in a large bowl; mix well. Cover bowl, stand mixture for up to a week.

Cream butter with sugar in large bowl with electric mixer only until ingredients are combined. Beat in eggs one at a time, beat only until combined between each addition. Add creamed mixture to fruit mixture, mix well; mix in sifted flours in 2 lots.

Spread mixture evenly into deep 25cm square or deep 28cm round prepared cake pan. Bake in slow oven for about 5 hours.

China: "Naif", Villeroy and Boch

50

square or deep 23cm round prepared cake pan. Decorate with blanched almonds and cherries if desired. Bake in slow oven for 3½ to 4 hours.

CHRISTMAS PUDDING

250g butter, melted, cooled
3 eggs, lightly beaten
250g (4 cups) stale breadcrumbs
  lightly packed
¼ cup plain flour, sifted

Use half the remaining Basic Fruit Mixture for the pudding, add above ingredients, mix thoroughly.

This mixture can be steamed, but we found the boiled result superior. Boil in cloth for 4 hours. See page 54.

Serves 6 to 8.

FRUIT MINCE TARTS

Use the remaining Basic Fruit Mixture to make about 50 tarts.

PASTRY
1 cup plain flour
1 cup self-raising flour
½ cup cornflour
¼ cup custard powder
¼ cup icing sugar
250g butter
¼ cup iced water, approximately

Sift dry ingredients into bowl and rub in butter. Add enough water to make the ingredients just cling together. Knead lightly on floured surface until the mixture is smooth. Divide into 4 portions, cover in plastic wrap, refrigerate portions for 20 minutes.

Clockwise from left: Christmas Pudding; Moist Christmas Cake; Fruit Mince Tarts

Roll quarter of the pastry between 2 pieces of plastic wrap until about 2mm thick. Cut pastry into 7cm rounds, place rounds into patty pans. Fill pastry cases with about a tablespoon of the Basic Fruit Mixture. Cut narrow strips of pastry from scraps, twist pastry, place on top of fruit mixture.

Bake tarts in a moderate oven for about 15 to 20 minutes. Stand the tarts 5 minutes before removing from pans to cool on wire rack. Repeat the process with remaining pastry and Basic Fruit Mixture.

Top: Celebration Cake; bottom: Festive Fruit and Nut Cake

Platter: Mikasa Tableware; candle holder: Artiana Imports

FESTIVE FRUIT AND NUT CAKE

This cake will keep for up to 3 months if stored in the refrigerator.

125g glacé pineapple
125g glacé apricots
250g dates
125g red glacé cherries
125g green glacé cherries
125g whole blanched almonds
250g brazil nuts
2 eggs
½ cup brown sugar
2 teaspoons vanilla essence
1 tablespoon rum
90g butter
⅓ cup plain flour
¼ cup self-raising flour

Chop pineapple and apricots into pieces the same size as brazil nuts; leave remaining fruit and nuts whole. Combine all fruit and nuts in bowl. Beat eggs in small bowl with electric mixer until thick and creamy, add sugar, essence, rum and softened butter, beat until combined. Stir into fruit mixture with sifted flours.

Spread mixture evenly and firmly into 14cm x 21cm loaf pan which has been greased and base-lined. Bake in slow oven for about 2 hours.

CELEBRATION CAKE

500g (3¼ cups) sultanas
250g (1½ cups) chopped raisins
250g (1½ cups) chopped dates
125g (¾ cup) currants
125g (½ cup) mixed peel
125g (⅔ cup) quartered glacé cherries
¼ cup chopped glacé pineapple
¼ cup chopped glacé apricots
½ cup rum
250g butter
1 cup brown sugar, firmly packed
5 eggs
1½ cups plain flour
⅓ cup self-raising flour
1 teaspoon mixed spice

Combine fruit in large bowl with rum. Cover, stand overnight or up to a week. Beat butter until soft, add sugar, beat only until combined. Add eggs one at a time, beat only until combined. Add creamed mixture to fruit mixture, mix well. Stir in sifted dry ingredients. Spread evenly into a deep 19cm square or a deep 23cm round prepared cake pan. Bake in a slow oven for 3 to 3½ hours.

FAVOURITE BOILED FRUIT CAKE

This is a rich boiled fruit cake that will keep well for at least 3 months. It is suitable to use as a wedding cake.

375g (2¼ cups) sultanas
250g (1½ cups) chopped raisins
250g (1½ cups) currants
125g (½ cup) mixed peel
125g (⅔ cup) halved glacé cherries
¼ cup chopped glacé pineapple
¼ cup glacé apricots
250g butter
1 cup brown sugar, firmly packed
½ cup brandy
½ cup water
5 eggs, lightly beaten
1 tablespoon treacle
2 teaspoons grated orange rind
1 teaspoon grated lemon rind
1¾ cups plain flour
⅓ cup self-raising flour
½ teaspoon bicarbonate of soda

Combine fruit, butter, sugar, brandy and water in saucepan. Stir constantly over heat without boiling until sugar is dissolved. Bring to the boil, reduce heat, simmer covered 10 minutes. Transfer to a large bowl and cool to room temperature.

Add eggs, treacle and rinds to fruit mixture, stir until combined. Stir in sifted dry ingredients. Spread mixture evenly into a deep 19cm square or a deep 23cm round prepared cake pan. Bake in slow oven for about 2½ hours.

GOLDEN FRUIT CAKE

250g butter
1 teaspoon grated lemon rind
1 cup castor sugar
4 eggs
250g (1½ cups) sultanas
125g (½ cup) mixed peel
60g (½ cup) slivered almonds
125g (⅔ cup) glacé cherries, quartered
125g (½ cup) chopped glacé pineapple
125g (½ cup) chopped glacé apricots
125g (½ cup) chopped glacé ginger
1½ cups plain flour

Cream butter, lemon rind and sugar in small bowl with electric mixer, beat until light and fluffy. Beat in eggs one at a time. Transfer to large bowl, stir in fruit mixture, then sifted flour. Spread

Plates: Corso Di Fiori

mixture evenly into a deep 20cm round prepared cake pan. Bake in a slow oven for about 3 hours.

MELT AND MIX FRUIT CAKE

We used a Granny Smith apple.

1½ kg mixed fruit, chopped
½ cup rum
1 apple, coarsely grated
1 tablespoon honey or golden syrup
1 cup brown sugar, firmly packed
4 eggs
250g butter, melted
1½ cups plain flour
½ cup self-raising flour
1 teaspoon mixed spice

Place mixed fruit in large bowl, then add rum, apple, honey, sugar and eggs and mix well. Stir in cooled butter, sift-

Clockwise from top left: Favourite Boiled Fruit Cake; Golden Fruit Cake; Melt and Mix Fruit Cake

ed flours and mixed spice. Spread the mixture evenly into a deep 19cm square or deep 23cm round prepared cake pan. Bake in slow oven for 3 to 3½ hours.

53

FAVOURITES

HOW TO BOIL AND STEAM PUDDINGS

These 2 recipes have become our most requested and favourite over the years. Both can be boiled or steamed, however, the methods accompanying each of the puddings give a slightly better result than the alternative method. The puddings can both be frozen, but there is no need to do this if they are stored correctly. They are not suitable to microwave.

To boil pudding: Dip prepared pudding cloth into boiling water; use rubber gloves to protect hands, wring excess water from cloth. Have ⅓ cup plain flour close to cloth. Spread hot cloth out on bench, quickly rub flour

into cloth to cover an area about 38cm in diameter **(above)**, leave flour thicker in the centre of the cloth, where the skin will need to be thickest.

Place cloth on bench, place mixture in centre of cloth. Gather ends of cloth together, hold pudding up, pat into shape with hand **(above)**.

Tie pudding securely with string, as close to pudding mixture as possible. Tie loop in string to make pudding easier to lift from the water. Pull ends of cloth tightly to make sure pudding is as round as possible. Have ready a large boiler three-quarters full of rapidly boiling water. Gently and quickly lower pudding into water, quickly replace lid, boil rapidly for specified cooking time. Replenish boiler with boiling water as it

evaporates; a tight-fitting lid will minimise evaporation of water. It is also a good idea to weight the lid with a brick or something similar. There must be enough water in the boiler for the pudding to move freely and the water should be deep enough for the pudding to float at all times.

After required cooking time, use handle of wooden spoon to lift pudding from water; place handle through looped string. Lift carefully but quickly from water; do not put pudding down as it is too soft at this stage. Suspend the pudding from a drawer or a cupboard handle.

It is important that the pudding can swing freely without touching anything. Twist ends of cloth around supporting string to keep wet ends away from pudding. If pudding has been cooked correctly, the cloth will begin to dry out in patches within a few minutes. Leave pudding to dry overnight. Next day, when pudding is cold, remove from handle, cut string, loosen cloth from top of pudding, scrape away any excess flour, leave at room temperature for a day or so (time will depend on humidity of the weather) or until the cloth is completely dry around the top of the pudding. Tie pudding cloth again with string, place pudding in airtight plastic bag, refrigerate until required.

To serve pudding hot: Remove pudding from refrigerator about 12 hours before it is to be reheated. Prepare for reheating the pudding about 3 hours before it is to be served.

Have large boiler three-quarters full of boiling water, gently lower pudding into boiler, boil for 1 to 2 hours depending on the size of the pudding. Suspend hot pudding for 10 minutes, tuck ends of cloth into string, away from top of pudding.

Have serving plate and scissors ready. Place pudding on bench, near to plate, cut string quickly, gently ease cloth away from pudding until about a quarter of the pudding is uncovered. Using a towel to protect hands, gently invert pudding onto serving plate; slowly and gently pull cloth away.

Leave pudding further 20 minutes before cutting. The longer the pudding is left standing, the darker the 'skin' will become.

To serve pudding cold: Reheat pudding the day before it is to be served. Proceed as above, then leave pudding to become completely cold, this will take at least 12 hours; cover with plastic food wrap, refrigerate pudding; or the cloth can be removed after the initial cooking. Allow the hot pudding to hang for 10 minutes then remove the

China: Lifestyle Imports "Taitu"; linen: Studio Haus; candle holder and bowl: Artiana Imports

cloth as instructed above. This is also the best method if a new cloth is to be used to give the pudding away as a gift. In this case, let the pudding become cold, then use a clean, dry, unfloured cloth, tie in position around the pudding as instructed above.

Pudding cloth: Buy half a metre of unbleached calico 122cm wide; cut in half, trim to give 2 square cloths. Soak calico in cold water overnight. Next day, boil for 20 minutes, then rinse well. Cloth is now ready for use. After pudding has been reheated and removed from cloth, soak cloth in cold water, boil and rinse well. Avoid using detergents for washing the cloth.

To steam pudding: Fill the pudding

mixture into well-greased aluminium steamer, cover with a large piece of foil.

Put lid firmly on steamer, then crush surplus foil firmly around the lid to help form a good seal. A china or enamel bowl of appropriate size can also be used; cover top with a double sheet of foil. Tie in position with string.

Place pudding in large boiler with enough boiling water to come halfway up side of steamer. Cover with tight-fitting lid, replenish boiling water as necessary during cooking time.

When cold, store pudding in steamer in refrigerator for up to 6 weeks. If storage time is to be any longer, remove the pudding from the steamer af-ter 10 minutes, cool to room tempera-ture, wrap in plastic wrap or bag then foil, store in refrigerator.

BOILED CHRISTMAS PUDDING

250g (1½ cups) raisins, chopped
250g (1½ cups) sultanas
185g (1 cup) currants
185g (¾ cup) mixed peel
1 teaspoon grated lemon rind
2 tablespoons lemon juice
2 tablespoons brandy
250g butter
500g (2 cups) brown sugar, firmly packed
5 eggs
1¼ cups plain flour

Left: Boiled Christmas Pudding; right: Steamed Christmas Pudding

½ teaspoon ground nutmeg
½ teaspoon mixed spice
250g (4 cups) stale breadcrumbs, lightly packed

Combine fruit, rind, juice and brandy in large bowl, mix well. Cover, stand over-night or up to a week.

Beat butter and sugar in large bowl with electric mixer only until combined. Beat in eggs one at a time, beat only until combined between each addition. Add creamed mixture to fruit mixture, sifted dry ingredients and bread-crumbs; mix well.

Boil pudding for 6 hours.

STEAMED CHRISTMAS PUDDING

500g (3¼ cups) mixed fruit, chopped
125g (¾ cup) chopped dates
125g (¾ cup) chopped raisins
1 cup water
1 cup brown sugar, lightly packed
125g butter
1 teaspoon bicarbonate of soda
2 eggs, lightly beaten
1 cup plain flour
1 cup self-raising flour
1 teaspoon mixed spice
½ teaspoon ground cinnamon
2 tablespoons dark rum

Combine fruit, water, sugar and butter in saucepan. Stir constantly over heat until butter is melted and sugar dissolved. Bring to the boil, reduce heat, simmer uncovered 8 minutes, stir in soda. Transfer mixture to a large bowl, stir in eggs, sifted dry ingredients and rum.

Place mixture into a well-greased 10 cup steamer or basin, steam for 5 hours.

SAUCES FOR THE PUDDING

Some people like cream and/or ice-cream with hot or cold pudding, others like it with a lavish sauce — we've given you a wide choice of hot and cold sauces and 2 delicious butters.

ORANGE LIQUEUR CUSTARD

Custard can be made the day before required and refrigerated. Reheat custard gently when required. Cointreau and Grand Marnier are citrus-flavoured liqueurs. This recipe is not suitable to freeze.

2 tablespoons custard powder
¼ cup sugar
½ cup orange juice
1 cup water
¼ cup sour cream
1 teaspoon grated orange rind
1 tablespoon Cointreau or Grand Marnier

Combine custard powder and sugar in saucepan, gradually stir in orange juice and water. Stir constantly over heat until mixture boils and thickens (or microwave on HIGH for about 5 minutes). Stir in sour cream, orange rind and liqueur, serve hot.

Makes about 2 cups.

CINNAMON BRANDY SAUCE

Serve sauce hot with cold whipped cream. This recipe is not suitable to freeze.

2 teaspoons ground cinnamon
3 teaspoons arrowroot
3 tablespoons sugar

1½ cups water
¼ cup brandy
15g butter

Combine cinnamon, arrowroot and sugar in saucepan, gradually stir in water, stir until smooth. Stir constantly over heat until sauce boils and thickens, reduce heat, simmer uncovered for 2 minutes (or microwave on HIGH for about 2 minutes). Stir in the brandy and butter.

Makes about 2 cups.

RUM CREAM SAUCE

This sauce can be made up to 2 days ahead and kept covered in the refrigerator. This sauce recipe is not suitable to freeze.

125g packet cream cheese, softened
30g soft butter
1 cup icing sugar
1 egg
1 teaspoon lemon juice
300ml carton thickened cream
2 tablespoons dark rum

Beat cream cheese and butter in a small bowl with electric mixer until light and creamy. Beat in sifted icing sugar, egg and lemon juice. Transfer mixture to large bowl, fold in whipped cream and rum. Refrigerate for several hours before serving.

Makes about 3 cups.

CREPE SUZETTE BUTTER

Cointreau and Grand Marnier are both citrus-flavoured liqueurs.

This delicious butter can be piped onto trays and refrigerated until set, then served on the hot pudding. It can be made 2 days in advance and stored covered in refrigerator. The butter can be frozen (piped if you prefer) for about 3 months.

125g soft unsalted butter
¼ cup icing sugar
1 teaspoon grated lemon rind
1 teaspoon grated orange rind
1 tablespoon lemon juice
2 tablespoons orange juice
1 tablespoon Cointreau or Grand Marnier

Beat the butter in a small bowl with an electric mixer, until it is soft and creamy and beat in the sifted icing sugar and rinds. Gradually beat in the juices and liqueur. Refrigerate butter until firm.

HARD SAUCE

Flavour the sauce with brandy, rum, whisky or sherry or any of your favourite liqueurs. Any citrus juice can be substituted. Make the sauce about a week ahead if desired and keep it cov-

ered in the refrigerator. Sauce can be frozen for about 3 months.

125g soft unsalted butter
2 cups icing sugar
1 tablespoon brandy

Cream butter in small bowl with electric mixer until light and fluffy, beat in sifted icing sugar and brandy. Refrigerate until firm. The butter can be put into a piping bag fitted with a fluted tube and piped into rosettes on tray.

Refrigerate until firm, or butter can be served by the spoonful onto servings of hot pudding.

CREME ANGLAISE

Sauce can be made 2 days before required and kept covered in refrigerator. This recipe is not suitable to freeze or microwave.

¼ cup castor sugar
4 egg yolks
1½ cups milk
1 teaspoon vanilla essence
2 teaspoons cornflour
2 teaspoons water
¼ cup cream

Combine sugar and egg yolks in small bowl, beat with electric mixer until thick and creamy. Place milk and essence in saucepan, bring to the boil. Remove from heat, gradually whisk into egg mixture. Return milk mixture to saucepan, stir constantly over low heat without boiling until custard thickens slightly. Blend cornflour with water, stir into custard, stir constantly over heat until mixture boils and thickens. Remove from heat, stir in cream; cool to room temperature.

Makes 2 cups.

CREAMY CUSTARD SAUCE

Sauce can be made 2 days ahead and kept covered in refrigerator. Flavour it with 2 tablespoons of liqueur, folded in with the cream. This recipe is not suitable to freeze or microwave.

¼ cup sugar
½ cup water
2 egg yolks
½ cup thickened cream

Combine sugar and water in saucepan, stir constantly over heat, without boiling until sugar is dissolved. Bring to the boil, reduce heat, simmer uncovered for about 7 minutes, or until sugar syrup is reduced to about ¼ cup. Beat egg yolks in small bowl with electric mixer until thick and creamy, gradually beat in hot sugar syrup in a thin stream, beat until mixture is thick and creamy. Fold in lightly whipped cream. Refrigerate until ready to serve.

Makes about 2 cups.

·GIFTS· TO SAVOUR

Make or bake delicious edible gifts for friends and family. We've included some special cakes, biscuits, chutneys, pickles and confectionery.

Marble table: Appley Hoare Antiques; basket: Swatow Imports; teatowel: Accoutrement

From right to left: Mango Passionfruit Butter; Lime Butter; Passionfruit Butter

GIFTS TO SAVOUR

BUTTERS

Store butters in the refrigerator for up to 3 weeks.

When making butters, it is important to stir the mixture constantly until it thickens slightly. Remember the butter will set in the recipe when it is cold. Do not have the simmering water touching the base of the bowl or base of the top part of the double saucepan.

MANGO PASSIONFRUIT BUTTER

This butter recipe is not suitable to freeze or microwave.

1 ripe mango
¼ cup passionfruit pulp
1 tablespoon grated lemon rind
¼ cup lemon juice
125g unsalted butter, chopped
⅓ cup sugar
4 eggs, lightly beaten

Mash mango pulp, place in top part of double saucepan or heatproof bowl. Stir in passionfruit, lemon rind and juice, butter, sugar and eggs. Stir constantly over simmering water until mixture thickens. Pour into hot sterilised jars; seal when cold.

Makes about 3 cups.

LIME BUTTER

Lemons can be substituted for limes when limes are not in season. You will need about 5 limes for this butter. This recipe is not suitable to freeze or microwave.

2 eggs, lightly beaten
½ cup sugar
1 tablespoon grated lime rind
½ cup lime juice
60g unsalted butter, chopped

Combine eggs and sugar in top part of double saucepan or heatproof bowl. Stir in rind, juice and butter, stir constantly over simmering water until mixture thickens. Pour into hot sterilised jars; seal when cold.

Makes about 1 cup.

PASSIONFRUIT BUTTER

This butter recipe is not suitable to freeze or microwave.

4 eggs, lightly beaten
¾ cup sugar
¼ cup lemon juice
⅓ cup passionfruit pulp
125g unsalted butter, chopped

Combine eggs and sugar in top of double saucepan or heatproof bowl. Stir in lemon juice, passionfruit and butter. Stir constantly over simmering water until mixture thickens. Pour into hot sterilised jars; seal when cold.

Makes about 2 cups.

APRICOT BUTTER

This butter recipe is not suitable to freeze or microwave.

250g (1½ cups) dried apricots, chopped
2 cups sugar
4 egg yolks
125g unsalted butter, chopped
2 tablespoons Grand Marnier
1 tablespoon grated lemon rind
1 tablespoon lemon juice

Cover apricots with boiling water, stand 30 minutes or until apricots are soft. Cook, covered in saucepan until soft, drain. Blend or process apricots until smooth.

Combine sugar and egg yolks in top part of double saucepan or heatproof bowl. Stir in remaining ingredients, stir constantly over simmering water until mixture thickens. Pour into hot sterilised jars; seal when cold.

Makes about 2½ cups.

JAMS

Jams and jellies make wonderful gifts which can be made a long time in advance to save a last minute panic.

There are a few important points to remember for success.
● Choose firm, unblemished, slightly under-ripe fruit.
● Cover and simmer the fruit mixture gently before sugar is added to minimise evaporation and allow the pectin to be extracted from the fruit.
● Once the sugar has been added to the fruit mixture it must not be more than 5cm deep, so choose a boiler or saucepan that will accommodate the jam mixture correctly.
● Boil the mixture rapidly uncovered after sugar is added for maximum evaporation. The faster the jam cooks at this stage the better it will be. This is the reason for using large, wide-topped pans.
● Stir constantly to dissolve sugar before the mixture boils.
● Do not stir the mixture while the jam is boiling. An occasional gentle stir simply to check the jam is not sticking to the base of the pan towards the end of the cooking time is fine.
● To test when jam is ready, it should be reduced by about half the original amount of mixture; it should fall in heavy drops from a wooden spoon,

and should feel like it will stick to the base of the pan. At this stage, remove the pan from the heat, allow the bubbles to subside, drop a teaspoon of the jam onto a refrigerator-cold saucer. Let the jam set at room temperature for accurate assessing. If the jam is like a marmalade — that is with fruit suspended in jelly — or it is a fruit jelly, push the jam on the saucer with your finger; it should have a skin which will wrinkle when it is pushed. Other jams — like pickles and chutneys — should just set to a spreading consistency (see individual recipes).
● Always leave the jam off the heat until the test is completed. If it is not set sufficiently, return to the heat and boil, perhaps only for a few minutes, before testing again.
● Jars and non-metal lids must be clean — a dishwasher does a good job — or boil the jars for about 20 minutes. Use jars while hot for best results.

Tiles: Pazotti; jars: Swing Gifts and Artiana Imports

● Fill the jars to the top with jam and cover them loosely with a cloth to keep dust-free. When the jam is at room temperature it will have shrunk slightly from the top. Seal with a lid, melted paraffin wax or slightly dampened rounds of cellophane.

● Label, date and store jam in a cool dark place. The refrigerator is perfect for when the weather is hot and humid.

SUPERB FOUR FRUIT JAM

We used Granny Smith apples in this recipe. This recipe is not suitable to freeze or microwave.

1 large grapefruit
1 large orange
1 large lemon
2 large apples
3 litres (12 cups) water
3kg (12 cups) sugar
1 teaspoon vinegar
1 teaspoon salt

Cut unpeeled fruit in half, slice fruit thinly, discard seeds. Place fruit in large bowl with water, cover, stand mixture overnight.

Next day, place fruit and water mixture into large boiler, bring to the boil, reduce heat, simmer covered for about 1 hour or until rind is transparent. Add sugar, stir constantly over heat, without boiling, until sugar is dissolved. Bring to the boil, boil rapidly uncovered, without stirring, for about 45 minutes or until jam will jell when tested on a cold saucer. Stir in vinegar and salt, stand 10 minutes. Pour into hot sterilised jars; seal when cold.

Makes about 4 cups.

OVERNIGHT PROCESSOR MARMALADE

This easy-to-make marmalade eliminates the need for hours of cutting fruit finely. This recipe is not suitable to freeze or microwave.

From left to right: Apricot Butter; Superb Four Fruit Jam; Overnight Processor Marmalade; Mandarin and Apricot Jam

1 large grapefruit, chopped
1 lemon, chopped
2 large oranges, chopped
1 litre (4 cups) water
1¾kg (7 cups) sugar

Blend or process fruit finely (seeds and all) in batches. Combine fruit and water in large boiler, bring to the boil, reduce heat, simmer covered 30 minutes, stand overnight.

Next day, bring mixture to the boil, add sugar, stir constantly over heat, without boiling, until sugar is dissolved. Boil rapidly, uncovered, without stirring, for about 30 minutes or until jam will jell when tested on a cold saucer. Stand 5 minutes, pour into hot sterilised jars; seal when cold.

Makes about 6 cups.

MANDARIN AND APRICOT JAM

This recipe is not suitable to freeze or microwave.

4 mandarins
1 lemon
250g (1½ cups) dried apricots, chopped
1¼kg (5 cups) water
1½kg (6 cups) sugar, approximately

Peel rind from mandarins and lemon with a vegetable peeler, taking care not to remove any pith with the rind. Shred rind finely. Remove membrane from mandarins and lemon, chop fruit roughly, discarding seeds. Place rind, chopped fruit, apricots and water in boiler. Bring to the boil, reduce heat, simmer covered for about 45 minutes or until rind is transparent. Measure mandarin mixture, allowing 1 cup sugar to each 1 cup of mixture. Return mandarin mixture to boiler with sugar, stir constantly over heat, without boiling, until sugar is dissolved. Boil uncovered, without stirring, for about 10 minutes or until jam will jell when tested on a cold saucer. Pour into hot, sterilised jars; seal when cold.

Makes about 7 cups.

QUICK AND EASY ORANGE JAM

This recipe is not suitable to freeze or microwave.

4 large oranges
1 litre (4 cups) water
750g (3 cups) sugar, approximately
1 tablespoon brandy

Peel oranges thickly to remove all white pith, discard skins. Chop oranges roughly, discard seeds. Combine orange pulp and water in boiler, cover, bring to the boil, reduce heat, simmer 20 minutes or until pulp is just tender. Measure orange mixture, allow ¾ cup sugar to each 1 cup of mixture. Return orange mixture and sugar to boiler, stir over heat, without boiling, until sugar is dissolved. Boil rapidly uncovered, without stirring, for about 20 minutes or until jam will jell when tested on a cold saucer. Stand 5 minutes, stir in brandy, pour into hot sterilised jars; seal when cold.

Makes about 3 cups.

RHUBARB AND APPLE JAM

This jam is more like a spread; the fruit does not set in a jelly-like marmalade. This recipe is not suitable to freeze or microwave.

500g (about 10 stalks) rhubarb
1kg (about 6 large) apples, peeled, sliced

½ cup water
½ cup lemon juice
1kg (4 cups) sugar, approximately

Place rhubarb and apples in boiler with water and lemon juice. Bring to the boil, reduce heat, simmer covered for about 20 minutes or until fruit is pulpy. Measure fruit mixture, allow ¾ cup sugar to each 1 cup fruit mixture. Return fruit mixture and sugar to boiler, stir constantly over high heat, without boiling, until sugar is dissolved. Boil uncovered, without stirring, for about 10 minutes or until jam will set to a spreading consistency when tested on a cold saucer. Pour into hot sterilised jars; seal when cold.

Makes about 6 cups.

GRAPEFRUIT AND TOMATO JAM

This recipe is not suitable to freeze or microwave.

2 grapefruit, sliced
1½ litres (6 cups) water
1kg (about 6) ripe firm tomatoes, peeled, chopped
2kg (8 cups) sugar, approximately

Reserve grapefruit seeds, tie in piece of cloth. Combine grapefruit, water and seeds in boiler. Cover, bring to the boil, reduce heat, simmer covered 45 minutes or until rind is tender. Add tomatoes, cover, simmer 30 minutes or until tomatoes are pulpy.

Measure mixture, allow 1 cup sugar to each 1 cup of mixture. Return mixture to boiler with sugar. Stir constantly over heat, without boiling, until sugar is dissolved, bring to the boil. Boil rapidly uncovered for about 30 minutes or until the jam will jell when tested on a cold saucer. Stand for 5 minutes before pouring into hot sterilised jars; seal when cold.

Makes about 8 cups.

PASSIONFRUIT SKIN JAM

This recipe is not suitable to freeze or microwave.

12 passionfruit
1½ litres (6 cups) water
⅓ cup lemon juice
2 cups sugar, approximately

Wash passionfruit well, discard stems. Remove pulp from passionfruit and reserve; this is added to the jam later. Place skins in large saucepan, add water and lemon juice, cover, bring to the boil, reduce heat, simmer covered for about 30 minutes or until inside of skins are puffy and changed in colour to burgundy and soft enough to remove from the outer layer. Drain, taking care to reserve liquid.

Scrape all skins with a teaspoon

until they are free from pulp, discard outer skins. Measure pulp, allow 1 cup sugar to each 1 cup of pulp. Return pulp and sugar to saucepan with reserved liquid. Stir constantly over heat, without boiling, until sugar is dissolved. Boil rapidly uncovered, without stirring, for about 30 minutes or until mixture sets to a spreading consistency when tested on a cold saucer. Add reserved passionfruit pulp, stand 10 minutes before pouring into hot sterilised jars; seal when cold.

Makes about 3 cups.

Table: Appley Hoare Antiques; clip top jars: H.A.C.; lidded jar and teatowel: Accoutrement

TOMATO PASSIONFRUIT AND APPLE JAM

We used Granny Smith apples in this recipe. This recipe is not suitable to freeze or microwave.

2 ripe firm tomatoes, peeled, chopped
2 apples, peeled, grated
¾ cup (about 8) passionfruit pulp
½ cup water
2 cups sugar, approximately

Combine the fruit and water in a large saucepan, cover and bring to the boil. Reduce heat and simmer 15 minutes or until apple is tender.

Measure the fruit mixture, allowing 1 cup of sugar to each 1 cup of mixture, return fruit and sugar to the saucepan. Stir constantly over heat, without boiling, until the sugar is dissolved. Boil uncovered, without stirring, for about 15 minutes or until jam will jell when tested on a cold saucer. Stand for a few minutes before pouring the jam into hot sterilised jars; seal when cold.

Makes about 3 cups.

Back: left to right: Quick and Easy Orange Jam; Apricot Amaretto Conserve; centre: left to right: Grapefruit and Tomato Jam; Rhubarb and Apple Jam; Pawpaw and Pineapple Jam; front: left: Passionfruit Skin Jam; right: Tomato Passionfruit and Apple Jam

PAWPAW AND PINEAPPLE JAM

This recipe is not suitable to freeze or microwave

2 firm pawpaws
1 pineapple
125g (½ cup) chopped glacé ginger
2 cups lemon juice
2kg (8 cups) sugar

Quarter, seed and peel pawpaws, chop into 2cm pieces. Peel pineapple, remove core, chop pineapple into 2cm pieces. Combine pawpaw, pineapple, ginger and lemon juice in boiler, cover, bring to the boil, reduce heat, simmer uncovered for 5 minutes. Add sugar, stir constantly over heat, without boiling, until sugar is dissolved. Bring to the boil, boil uncovered, without stirring, for about 30 minutes or until jam will jell when tested on a cold saucer. Stand 5 minutes before pouring into hot sterilised jars; seal when cold.

Makes about 12 cups.

APRICOT AMARETTO CONSERVE

The dried apricots need to be soaked overnight for best results. Amaretto is an almond-flavoured liqueur. This recipe is not suitable to freeze or microwave.

250g (1½ cups) dried apricots
1½ cups water
2 teaspoons grated orange rind
1 cup orange juice
2 tablespoons lemon juice
1¼ cups sugar
½ cup slivered almonds
2 tablespoons Amaretto

Cut apricots into thin strips, combine with water in bowl, cover, stand the mixture overnight.

Combine apricots, water and rind in saucepan, bring to the boil, reduce heat, simmer uncovered 10 minutes or until apricots are soft. Add juices and sugar, stir constantly over heat, without boiling, until sugar is dissolved. Bring to the boil, reduce heat, simmer uncovered for 30 minutes or until jam will jell when tested on a cold saucer. Stir in almonds and liqueur. Pour into hot sterilised jars; seal when cold.

Makes about 2½ cups.

APPLE PASSIONFRUIT JELLY

Use any variety of apples for this recipe. This recipe is not suitable to freeze or microwave.

1kg (about 6 large) apples
1½ litres (6 cups) water
1kg (4 cups) sugar, approximately
½ cup passionfruit pulp

Cut unpeeled apples thinly crossways

ABOVE:
Mandarin
Marmalade
LEFT:
Apple
Passionfruit
Jelly

into slices. Combine the apples (including cores and seeds) and water in boiler. Cover, bring to the boil, reduce heat and simmer 1 hour. Strain mixture through a fine well-wrung out, damp cloth; allow mixture to drip through cloth for several hours or preferably overnight. Do not squeeze or press the mixture through the cloth as this will result in a cloudy jelly.

Measure the strained liquid, discard the apple pulp. Add ¾ cup sugar to each 1 cup of liquid; return liquid and sugar to the boiler. Stir liquid constantly over heat, without boiling, until the sugar is dissolved. Bring to the boil, boil rapidly uncovered for about 15 minutes or until the mixture will jell when tested on a cold saucer. Gently stir passionfruit through jelly then stand 5 minutes. Pour into hot sterilised jars; seal when cold.

Makes about 3½ cups.

MANDARIN MARMALADE

This recipe is unsuitable to freeze or microwave.

2kg (about 8) large mandarins
1kg (4 cups) sugar
3 cups water
2 tablespoons brandy

Peel mandarins, discard half the skins, finely slice remaining skins. Cut mandarins horizontally in half, discard seeds. Blend or process mandarin pulp in batches until chopped, combine rind, pulp, sugar and water in boiler. Stir constantly over heat, without boiling, until sugar is dissolved. Bring to the boil, reduce heat, simmer uncovered, without stirring, for about 50 minutes or until mixture will jell when tested on a cold saucer. Stir in brandy, stand 10 minutes, pour into hot sterilised jars; seal when cold.

Makes about 5 cups.

BISCUITS

LEMON STARS

The biscuits can be made up to a week ahead and stored in an airtight container; they can be frozen for up to 2 months. This recipe is not suitable to microwave.

125g butter
¼ cup castor sugar
1 cup plain flour
½ cup cornflour

LEMON ICING
2 cups icing sugar
1 teaspoon butter
2 tablespoons lemon juice
red and green food colouring
silver cachous

Cream butter and sugar in small bowl with electric mixer until light and fluffy, gradually beat in sifted flours. Knead on lightly floured surface for about 5 minutes; kneading makes the cooked biscuit crisp. Roll pastry to about 2mm thickness, cut into star shapes. Place onto lightly greased oven trays, bake in moderate oven for about 10 minutes or

Clockwise from top: Shortbread Fingers; Hazelnut Bread; Cheese Biscuits; Lemon Stars

until lightly browned. Lift onto wire rack to cool. Spread biscuits with icing, decorate with silver cachous.

Lemon Icing: Sift icing sugar into a heatproof bowl, add butter and lemon juice. Stir over hot water until icing is spreadable. Tint icing with food colouring and use immediately.

Makes about 24.

63

GIFTS TO SAVOUR

SHORTBREAD FINGERS

Shortbread can be stored in an airtight container for up to 2 weeks or frozen for up to 2 months. This recipe is not suitable to microwave.

250g butter
⅓ cup castor sugar
2¼ cups plain flour
¼ cup rice flour (or ground rice)
1 tablespoon castor sugar, extra

Cream butter and sugar in small bowl with electric mixer until light and fluffy. Stir in sifted flours in 2 lots, knead lightly until smooth on a lightly floured surface. Press mixture over base of 19cm x 29cm lamington pan, prick well with a fork, sprinkle with extra sugar. Bake in slow oven for about 40 minutes or until lightly browned. Stand few minutes, cut into fingers, cool in pan.

HAZELNUT BREAD

This bread can be kept in an airtight container for a month. It is not suitable to freeze or microwave.

3 egg whites
½ cup castor sugar
1 cup plain flour
185g (1½ cups) whole roasted hazelnuts

Beat egg whites in small bowl with electric mixer until soft peaks form, gradually add sugar, beat for about 5 minutes or until sugar is dissolved. Fold in sifted flour and nuts. Spread mixture into greased and lined 8cm x 26cm bar pan. Bake in moderate oven for about 30 minutes or until firm to touch, turn onto wire rack to cool. When cold, wrap in foil, stand 1 to 2 days before slicing thinly. Place slices on oven trays in single layer. Bake slices in a moderate oven 10 minutes or until lightly browned and crisp.

Makes about 50.

CHEESE BISCUITS

Store the biscuits in an airtight container for up to a week. They can be frozen, unbaked, for up to 2 months. Cook frozen biscuits in a moderate oven for about 25 minutes. This recipe is not suitable to microwave.

1 cup plain flour
2 tablespoons self-raising flour
pinch cayenne pepper
125g butter
1 cup grated tasty cheese
2 tablespoons grated parmesan cheese
1 teaspoon French mustard
¼ cup lemon juice, approximately
1 tablespoon milk

Pecan Crunchies

1 tablespoon sesame seeds
1 tablespoon caraway seeds

Sift dry ingredients into bowl, rub in butter. Add cheeses, mustard and enough lemon juice to mix to a firm dough, knead on lightly floured surface until smooth. Place dough in centre of a sheet of plastic wrap, fold half the plastic over dough. Shape dough into a 30cm log, wrap; refrigerate for several hours. Cut dough into 5mm slices, place on lightly greased oven trays, brush with milk, sprinkle with seeds. Bake in moderate oven for about 15 minutes or until lightly browned. Stand 5 minutes before lifting onto wire racks to cool.

Makes about 24.

PECAN CRUNCHIES

Long, slow cooking makes these biscuits deliciously crunchy. The biscuits will keep in an airtight container for about 2 weeks; they can be frozen for about 2 months. This recipe is not suitable to microwave.

125g butter
⅔ cup raw sugar
2 tablespoons golden syrup
1 egg, lightly beaten
1 cup coconut
1½ cups wholemeal self-raising flour
100g (1 cup) pecans, approximately

Melt butter in saucepan, stir in sugar, golden syrup and egg, then coconut and flour. Using floured hands, roll teaspoonfuls of mixture into balls, place onto greased oven trays; allow for spreading. Press pecans on top to flatten biscuits slightly. Bake in slow oven for about 30 minutes or until golden brown. Cool on wire rack.

Makes about 20.

WHOLEMEAL SHORTBREAD

Shortbread will keep well in an airtight container for at least a month; it can also be frozen for 3 months. This recipe is not suitable to microwave.

250g butter
½ cup sugar
1¼ cups wholemeal plain flour
1¼ cups plain flour
½ cup rice flour (or ground rice)

1 Have butter at room temperature. Beat butter and sugar in small bowl with electric mixer, until pale and fluffy. Transfer to large bowl. Stir in the sifted dry ingredients in 2 lots to give a firm dough.

2 Turn dough onto lightly floured surface, knead lightly (over-handling will toughen the shortbread) until smooth. Roll dough to 1cm thickness. Cut into a 20cm round, using cake pan as a guide.

3 Place round of dough on lightly greased oven tray. Use thumb and forefinger of one hand and forefinger of the other to pinch a decorative border around the edge of the shortbread.

Wholemeal Shortbread

4 Mark shortbread into 12 sections with a large knife; do not cut through. Prick the top of each section with a fork. Bake in moderately slow oven for about 35 minutes or until lightly browned; cool on tray.

MUESLI SLICE

Slice will keep in an airtight container for up to 2 weeks; it can be frozen for up to 2 months. This recipe is not suitable to microwave.

125g butter
2 tablespoons honey
2 eggs, lightly beaten
½ cup raw sugar
1½ cups natural muesli
½ cup coconut
½ cup wholemeal plain flour
60g (½ cup) flaked almonds
125g (¾ cup) chopped raisins
¼ cup sesame seeds

Melt butter and honey in saucepan, remove from heat. Stir in eggs, sugar, muesli, coconut, flour, almonds, raisins and sesame seeds. Press mixture into greased 19cm x 29cm lamington pan. Bake in moderate oven for about 20 minutes. Cool in pan, cut when cold.

WHOLEMEAL APRICOT SLICE

This slice will keep in an airtight container for 2 weeks; it can be frozen for 2 months. This recipe is not suitable to microwave.

PASTRY
1½ cups wholemeal plain flour
1 cup wholemeal self-raising flour
125g butter
¼ cup milk
1 egg, lightly beaten
1 tablespoon honey
1 egg white
1 tablespoon castor sugar
FILLING
200g (1 cup) chopped dried apricots
1 cup water
2 teaspoons grated lemon rind
1 tablespoon lemon juice

Pastry: Combine sifted flours in large bowl, rub in butter. Stir in combined milk, egg and honey. Turn dough onto lightly floured surface, knead until smooth. Roll out half the pastry large enough to line base of a greased 19cm x 29cm lamington pan. Spread evenly with cold filling. Roll out remaining pastry large enough to cover filling. Brush lightly with egg white, sprinkle with sugar. Bake in moderately hot oven for 10 minutes, reduce heat to moderate, bake further 20 minutes. Cool in pan, cut when cold.

Filling: Combine all ingredients in saucepan, bring to the boil, reduce heat, simmer uncovered for about 10

Clockwise from back right: Muesli Slice; Honey Wholemeal Slice; Wholemeal Apricot Slice; Chocolate Oat Bars; Peanut Rough Slice

minutes or until liquid has evaporated; stir occasionally during cooking, cool to room temperature.

HONEY WHOLEMEAL SLICE

Slice will keep in an airtight container for up to 2 weeks: it can be frozen for up to 2 months. This recipe is not suitable to microwave.

125g butter
½ cup honey
⅓ cup brown sugar
1½ cups coconut
1½ cups rolled oats
155g (1 cup) sultanas
½ cup wholemeal self-raising flour
Combine butter, honey and sugar in saucepan, stir over low heat, without boiling, until the butter is melted and the sugar is dissolved.

Combine remaining ingredients in large bowl, stir in butter mixture. Press mixture evenly into a greased 19cm x 29cm lamington pan. Bake in moderate oven for about 20 minutes. Cool in pan, cut when cold.

CHOCOLATE OAT BARS

Milk bits are small buttons of milk chocolate. Bars will keep in an airtight container for 2 weeks; they can be frozen for 2 months. This recipe is not suitable to microwave.

1 cup rolled oats
1 cup plain flour
½ cup castor sugar
60g (½ cup) chopped pecans or walnuts
90g (½ cup) sultanas
½ cup Milk bits
125g butter, melted
2 tablespoons golden syrup
Combine oats, sifted flour, sugar, pecans, sultanas and Milk bits in large bowl, stir in butter and golden syrup. Press mixture into 19cm x 29cm lamington pan. Bake in moderate oven for about 25 minutes. Cool in pan, cut when cold.

PEANUT ROUGH SLICE

Slice will keep in an airtight container for up to 2 weeks; it can be frozen for up to 2 months. This recipe is not suitable to microwave.

1 cup plain flour
¼ cup self-raising flour
¾ cup rolled oats
90g (¾ cup) unsalted roasted peanuts
125g butter
¾ cup brown sugar, firmly packed
2 tablespoons honey
2 tablespoons peanut butter

Back: Cinnamon Almond Biscuits; front: Chocolate Fleck Cookies.

Combine sifted flours, oats and peanuts in large bowl. Combine butter, sugar, honey and peanut butter in saucepan, stir the mixture constantly over low heat for about 3 minutes or until the butter is melted, stir into the flour mixture until well combined.

Press into greased 19cm x 29cm lamington pan. Bake in moderate oven for about 25 minutes. Cool in pan, cut when cold.

CINNAMON ALMOND BISCUITS

Biscuits will keep in an airtight container for up to 2 weeks; they can be frozen for up to 2 months. This recipe is not suitable to microwave.

¾ cup plain flour
⅓ cup self-raising flour
1 teaspoon ground cinnamon
¼ cup castor sugar
¼ cup packaged ground almonds
125g butter
1 egg, separated
Sift flours, cinnamon, and sugar into a bowl, add almonds, rub in butter. Add egg yolk, mix ingredients together with hand. Knead gently and quickly on a lightly floured surface, until dough is smooth. If the weather is hot, wrap dough in plastic wrap and refrigerate for 30 minutes.

Roll dough to 5mm thickness and cut into 5cm rounds. Place on lightly greased oven trays and brush with egg white. Bake in a moderate oven for about 10 minutes, or until lightly browned. Lift onto wire rack to cool.

Makes about 24.

Clockwise from right: Hazelnut Crescents; Walnut Florentines; Spicy Fruit Scrolls; Cherry Macaroons; Buttery Nut Cookies

CHOCOLATE FLECK COOKIES

Biscuits will keep for up to 2 weeks in an airtight container; they can be frozen for 2 months. This recipe is not suitable to microwave.

125g butter
2 tablespoons castor sugar
½ cup sweetened condensed milk
1½ cups self-raising flour
75g dark chocolate, grated

Cream butter and sugar in small bowl with electric mixer until light and fluffy, beat in condensed milk, then sifted flour in 2 lots, stir in chocolate. Roll teaspoonfuls of mixture into balls, place on lightly greased oven trays, press down lightly with a fork. Bake in moderate oven for about 10 minutes.

Makes about 35.

HAZELNUT CRESCENTS

Crescents can be stored in an airtight container for about 3 weeks; they can be frozen for about 2 months. This recipe is not suitable to microwave.

1 cup plain flour
2 tablespoons castor sugar
125g butter
⅓ cup packaged ground roasted hazelnuts
1 egg yolk
icing sugar

Sift flour and castor sugar into bowl, rub in butter, mix in hazelnuts and egg yolk. Knead lightly on floured surface until smooth. Roll teaspoonfuls of mixture into 7cm long sausages, shape into crescents. Bake on lightly greased oven trays in moderately slow oven for

about 15 minutes or until lightly browned. Sift icing sugar over warm crescents, lift onto wire racks to cool.

Makes about 30.

WALNUT FLORENTINES

Store florentines in the refrigerator in an airtight container for up to a month. This recipe is not suitable to freeze or microwave.

½ cup castor sugar
½ cup wholemeal plain flour
2 teaspoons grated orange rind
60g (½ cup) finely chopped pecans or walnuts
1 cup thickened cream
200g dark chocolate

Combine sugar, sifted flour, rind and walnuts in bowl, gradually stir in cream.

Drop teaspoons of mixture onto greased oven trays, about 5cm apart. Bake in moderate oven for about 10 minutes or until golden brown around the edges. Loosen biscuits on tray immediately, then lift carefully onto wire racks to cool.

Melt chocolate over hot water, cool slightly. Spread chocolate onto flat side of biscuits, place onto trays, chocolate side up, refrigerate until the chocolate is set.

Makes about 80.

SPICY FRUIT SCROLLS

Cut the biscuits off the frozen rolls as required or bake as directed below. Biscuits will keep for at least 2 weeks in an airtight container. This recipe is not suitable to microwave.

250g butter
375g (2 cups) brown sugar, lightly packed
3 eggs
4½ cups plain flour
½ teaspoon ground cinnamon
½ teaspoon ground cardamom
1 teaspoon bicarbonate of soda
1 cup fruit mince
1 cup jam
Cream butter and sugar in large bowl with electric mixer until smooth; add eggs one at a time, beat until light and creamy. Stir in sifted dry ingredients in 2 batches, press into smooth ball. Divide dough into 4 rounds, refrigerate several hours.

Roll each round of dough on lightly floured surface to a 25cm x 35cm rectangle. Spread 2 rectangles with fruit mince, spread remaining 2 rectangles with jam. Roll both long sides of each rectangle towards centre, place rolls on tray, cover with plastic wrap, freeze several hours, or until firm.

Cut rolls into thick slices, place cut side up on lightly greased oven trays. Bake in moderate oven for about 10 minutes. Lift onto wire racks to cool.

Makes about 100.

CHERRY MACAROONS

These biscuits will keep well in an airtight container for about a month. This recipe is not suitable to freeze or microwave.

3 cups coconut
400g can sweetened condensed milk
200g (1 cup) red glacé cherries, finely chopped
1½ cups coconut, extra
Combine coconut, condensed milk and cherries. Roll teaspoonfuls of mixture into balls, toss in extra coconut. Place on oven trays covered with a

Decadent Chocolate Cookies

sheet of baking paper. Top biscuits with pieces of extra cherry if preferred. Bake in moderate oven for about 20 minutes. Lift onto wire racks to cool.

Makes about 50.

BUTTERY NUT COOKIES

Cookies will keep well in an airtight container for about 2 weeks; they can be frozen for 2 months. This recipe is not suitable to microwave.

250g butter
1 teaspoon vanilla essence
¾ cup castor sugar
1 egg yolk
2 cups plain flour
½ cup self-raising flour
125g (1¼ cups) pecans or blanched almonds, approximately
Beat butter, essence, sugar and egg yolk in small bowl with electric mixer until smooth and creamy. Transfer mixture to large bowl, stir in sifted flours in 2 lots. Divide mixture in half, roll each half into a sausage shape about 3cm in diameter, wrap in greaseproof or baking paper, refrigerate 30 minutes. Cut roll into 3mm slices, place onto lightly greased oven trays. Press a nut into each biscuit. Bake in moderate oven for about 10 minutes or until lightly browned. Cool on tray for a few minutes, then lift onto wire racks to cool.

Makes about 70.

DECADENT CHOCOLATE COOKIES

These super cookies have several kinds of chocolate and other goodies in them. Store cookies in an airtight container for up to a week. The centres of the baked cookies should be slightly soft and fudgy. Mix and match the nuts to suit individual tastes.

250g unsalted butter
100g dark chocolate, chopped
2 cups (375g) brown sugar, lightly packed
4 eggs, lightly beaten
2½ cups plain flour
⅓ cup cocoa
100g (1 cup) chopped pecans or walnuts
60g (½ cup) chopped roasted hazelnuts
90g (½ cup) sultanas
100g packet Choc bits
100g white chocolate, chopped
Melt butter and dark chocolate in large heatproof bowl over hot water. Stir in sugar and eggs, then sifted flour and cocoa, nuts, sultanas, Choc bits and white chocolate. Drop tablespoons of mixture into greased shallow round-based patty pans or onto lightly-greased oven trays. Bake in moderately hot oven 10 minutes, or until just set, lift onto wire racks to cool.

Makes about 50.

Table: Appley Hoare Antiques; cloth: Les Olivades; bowls: Kosta Boda 'Poem'

Clockwise from top: Chocolate Nut Truffles; Chocolate Nut Fudge; Chocolate-Topped Almond Macaroons

CONFECTIONERY

Confectionery is fun to make and give. Some of these recipes will be easier to make if a candy thermometer is used; a thermometer takes the guess work out of sweetsmaking.

When you buy a candy thermometer, test it for accuracy by placing it in a saucepan with enough cold water to cover the mercury. Bring the water to the boil and check that the thermometer registers 100°C (212°F) when the water is boiling.

When using the thermometer in a syrup, always bring the thermometer

to the boil in water, then place it in the syrup when it is boiling. When the required temperature has been reached, return the thermometer to a pan of boiling water, turn the water off and allow the thermometer to cool down with the water. With this care the thermometer should last for many years.

CHOCOLATE NUT TRUFFLES

Truffles can be made up to 2 months in advance and stored, covered, in the refrigerator. This recipe is not suitable to freeze.

¼ cup unroasted whole hazelnuts
½ cup thickened cream
125g dark chocolate, chopped
15g butter
1 teaspoon dark rum
¾ cup Rice Bubbles, finely chopped

Toast hazelnuts on oven tray in moderate oven 5 minutes, cool, chop finely.

Heat cream and chocolate in saucepan over low heat, stir until chocolate is melted (or microwave on HIGH for about 2 minutes), cool. Stir in butter and rum, refrigerate until mixture is cold. Beat chocolate mixture in small bowl with electric mixer until soft peaks form; do not overbeat. Refrigerate mixture until firm. Shape teaspoonfuls of mixture into balls, roll in combined hazelnuts and Rice Bubbles. Makes about 24.

CHOCOLATE NUT FUDGE

Fudge can be stored in an airtight container in the refrigerator for about 2 months. This recipe is not suitable to freeze.

200g packaged marshmallows
60g butter
1 tablespoon water
1 teaspoon vanilla essence
125g dark chocolate, chopped
125g (1 cup) chopped pecans or
**   walnuts**

Combine marshmallows, butter and water in saucepan, stir over low heat until butter and marshmallows are melted (or microwave on MEDIUM HIGH for about 2 minutes). Remove from heat, stir in essence and chocolate, beat with wooden spoon until mixture begins to thicken. Stir in nuts; mixture should be thick and sticky. Spread mixture into greased and foil-lined 8cm x 26cm bar pan. Refrigerate several hours before cutting.

CHOCOLATE-TOPPED ALMOND MACAROONS

Macaroons will keep well in an airtight container for a month. This recipe is not suitable to freeze or microwave.

60g dark chocolate, chopped
3 egg whites
¾ cup castor sugar
2 tablespoons packaged ground
**   almonds**
1½ cups coconut
125g dark chocolate, extra
flaked almonds

Melt chocolate over hot water, cool.

Beat egg whites in small bowl with electric mixer until soft peaks form, gradually add sugar, beat until dissolved. Stir in ground almonds, coconut and cooled chocolate; stand 10 minutes. Drop teaspoonfuls of mixture onto foil-covered trays, about 2cm apart. Bake in moderately slow oven for about 15 minutes, cool on trays. Melt extra chocolate over hot water, spread a little over each macaroon, top each with a flaked almond.

Makes about 40.

CHOCOLATE CARAMELS

Caramels can be stored in an airtight container in the refrigerator. This recipe is not suitable to freeze or microwave.

400g can sweetened condensed milk
2 tablespoons golden syrup
60g butter

TOPPING
90g dark chocolate, chopped
15g butter

Combine condensed milk and golden syrup in heavy-based saucepan; stir constantly over heat for about 10 minutes or until mixture turns golden brown. It will be necessary to reduce heat gradually as caramel is cooking; if heat is too high, caramel will burn. Remove from heat, add butter, stir until melted. Pour mixture into greased 8cm x 26cm bar pan, smooth top with wet fingers. When cold, spread with topping; refrigerate before cutting.
Topping: Melt chocolate over hot water, stir in butter.

BRANDY CREAM TRUFFLES

Truffles will keep stored in refrigerator for about 2 months. This recipe is not suitable to freeze.

250g dark chocolate, chopped
⅔ cup thickened cream
2 tablespoons brandy
30g butter, softened
cocoa

Melt chocolate over hot water. Heat cream in small saucepan until bubbles form around edge, quickly stir cream and brandy into chocolate. Refrigerate chocolate mixture until just firm enough to hold its shape. Beat butter in small bowl with electric mixer or wooden spoon until smooth, gradually beat in chocolate mixture. Spoon mixture into piping bag fitted with a fluted tube. Pipe mixture into small paper cases; refrigerate until set. Dust tops with sifted cocoa.

Makes about 30.

SESAME NUT CARAMELS

Store caramels in refrigerator for up to a month. This recipe is not suitable to freeze or microwave.

½ cup sesame seeds
1 cup castor sugar
90g butter
2 tablespoons golden syrup
⅓ cup liquid glucose
½ cup sweetened condensed milk
½ cup unsalted roasted peanuts,
**   chopped**

Place sesame seeds in saucepan, stir constantly over heat until seeds are lightly browned, then remove from pan to cool.

Combine sugar, butter, golden syrup, glucose and condensed milk in heavy-based saucepan, stir constantly over heat, without boiling, until sugar is dissolved. Bring to the boil, boil uncovered, stirring constantly, for 7 minutes or until light golden brown.

Stir in peanuts, pour immediately into greased 19cm x 29cm lamington pan, cool to lukewarm. Cut caramel into strips lengthways. Using hand, roll each strip on smooth surface to round off corners. Roll caramel rolls in sesame seeds to coat completely. Refrigerate until firm, cut into slices.

Makes about 60.

CHOCOLATE TOFFEE

Toffee can be stored in an airtight container in refrigerator for about 2 months. This recipe is not suitable to freeze or microwave.

2¼ cups sugar
⅔ cup water
125g butter
¼ teaspoon cream of tartar
125g dark chocolate, finely chopped

Combine sugar, water, butter and cream of tartar in saucepan, stir constantly over heat until sugar is dissolved. Bring to the boil, boil until mix-

ture reaches 160°C (320°F) on candy thermometer. Remove toffee from heat immediately, quickly stir in chocolate. Pour mixture into greased 19cm x 29cm lamington pan. When beginning to set, mark toffee into squares. When almost set, remove toffee from pan; cut into squares.

CHOCOLATE RUM CHERRIES

Store cherries in an airtight container in the refrigerator for up to a month. This recipe is not suitable to freeze or microwave.

125g (⅔ cup) glacé cherries
¼ cup dark rum
90g dark chocolate, chopped
60g (½ cup) chopped pecans or
   walnuts

Combine cherries and rum in bowl; stand overnight.

Melt chocolate over hot water. Drain cherries, pat dry with absorbent paper, coat each cherry in chocolate.

Place onto foil-covered tray, refrigerate until almost set. Roll cherries in walnuts, refrigerate until set.

Makes about 30.

PEPPERMINT MALLOWS

Store in an airtight container in the refrigerator for about 2 weeks. This recipe is not suitable to freeze or microwave.

2 cups sugar
¾ cup water
1 tablespoon liquid glucose
2 tablespoons gelatine
⅔ cup water, extra
1 egg white
peppermint essence
green food colouring

Grease a 19cm x 29cm lamington pan, dust with sifted icing sugar; shake out excess sugar.

Combine sugar and water in saucepan, stir constantly over heat, without boiling, until sugar is dissolved. Bring

Back, from left: Brandy Cream Truffles; Peppermint Mallows; Chocolate Rum Cherries; Chocolate Caramel; centre, from left: Chocolate Toffee; Sesame Nut Caramel

to the boil, add glucose, boil until mixture reaches 126°C (250°F) on candy thermometer. While syrup is reaching the correct temperature, sprinkle gelatine over extra water, dissolve over hot water. Place gelatine mixture into large bowl, gradually whisk in boiling sugar syrup in a thin stream. Beat egg white in small bowl with electric mixer until firm peaks form, gradually beat in gelatine-syrup in a thin stream, beating constantly. Beat until almost cold, add a drop of essence and colouring. Pour mixture into prepared pan, refrigerate until set, dust top lightly with some extra sifted icing sugar, turn out, cut into squares or fancy shapes, toss the shapes in icing sugar.

From left: Mint Leaf Christmas Tree; Chocolate Freckle Tree; White Chocolate Truffle Tree

WHITE CHOCOLATE TRUFFLE TREE

This recipe makes 1 Christmas tree. Truffles can be made up to a week before required. Store covered in refrigerator. Tree can be assembled up to a day ahead. This recipe is not suitable to freeze.

125g white chocolate, chopped
3 honey ice-cream cones
60g dark chocolate, chopped
TRUFFLES
200g white chocolate, chopped
125g packet cream cheese
1 tablespoon honey
1 teaspoon vanilla essence
¼ cup roasted unsalted peanuts, chopped
¼ cup coconut
1 cup coconut, extra

Melt white chocolate over hot water.
To form base: Mark a 6cm circle on a foil-covered tray, spread with a little of the white chocolate. Stack cones together using a small amount of white chocolate and secure to base. This forms the tree (cone) shape. Completely cover cone with a thin layer of white chocolate. Starting at the base of cone, place truffles around edge of cone, securing with a small amount of white chocolate. Continue in layers to form tree. Refrigerate until set. Melt dark chocolate over hot water, drizzle over tree. Refrigerate until required.

Truffles: Melt chocolate over hot water; cool. Beat chocolate, softened cream cheese, honey and essence in a small bowl with electric mixer until smooth. Stir in peanuts and coconut, cover, refrigerate several hours or until firm. Roll teaspoonfuls of the mixture into balls, toss in extra coconut, refrigerate until firm.

MINT LEAF CHRISTMAS TREES

This recipe makes 2 trees. Store trees in a cool place. Trees can be made up to 2 weeks ahead. This recipe is not suitable to freeze.

1 egg white
1½ cups pure icing sugar, approximately
6 honey ice-cream cones
400g mint leaf sweets
silver cachous

Place egg white in small bowl of electric mixer. Gradually beat in enough sifted icing sugar to give stiff spreadable consistency. Cover icing with damp cloth. Stack 3 cones together using a little icing between each. Repeat with remaining cones. Starting at base of cone, spread icing over one-third of the cone. Place a row of mint leaves around base of cone, overlapping the first layer. Spread remaining cone with icing. Continue arranging rows of mint leaves around cone until about 6 or 7 rows are formed. Leave a

little space at the top. Cover top with silver cachous. Repeat procedure with remaining icing, cones and leaves. Sift a little extra icing sugar over trees.

CHOCOLATE FRECKLE TREES

This recipe makes 2 trees. Trees can be made up to 2 weeks ahead; store in a cool place. This recipe is not suitable to freeze.

1 egg white
1½ cups pure icing sugar, approximately
green food colouring
6 honey ice-cream cones
250g chocolate freckles
small piece white cardboard
glue
silver glitter

Place egg white in small bowl of electric mixer. Gradually beat in enough sifted icing sugar to give a stiff spreadable consistency. Tint with food colouring. Cover icing with damp cloth. Stack 3 cones together using a little icing between each. Repeat with remaining cones. Spread icing evenly over cones. Place a row of freckles around base of cones, continue layering freckles, slightly over-lapping each layer, until cones are covered; leave space for stars. Cut star shapes out of cardboard, spread with glue, sprinkle with glitter. Spread back of stars with icing, place on trees.

CANDY CANES

Inexpensive and delicious treats for kids, candy canes can also be hung as decorations on the Christmas tree. Store in an airtight container for up to a month. This recipe is not suitable to freeze or microwave.

**1 cup sugar
1 tablespoon liquid glucose
¼ cup water
1 teaspoon brown vinegar
peppermint essence
red food colouring
green food colouring**

1 Combine sugar, glucose, water and vinegar in saucepan. Stir over heat, without boiling, until sugar is dissolved. Bring to the boil, without stirring. Boil rapidly, without stirring. Allow syrup to boil until a teaspoon of syrup becomes brittle when tested in cold water (or reaches 138°C (280°F) on a candy thermometer). Remove from heat, cool 3 minutes. Pour the toffee onto a lightly oiled marble slab or laminated surface. When toffee develops a slight skin, add a drop of peppermint essence. Using a spatula, turn edges of the mixture constantly towards the centre until mixture is cool enough to handle.

2 Lightly oil your hands and stretch the toffee into a long strip, fold the

Candy Canes

strip in half and twist together. Continue this stretching and twisting until the toffee becomes white. Stretch the toffee into a long strip about 1cm wide.

3 Using oiled scissors, cut toffee into 8 strips. With a paint brush paint a fine strip of red or green food colouring onto each toffee strip.

4 Twist each strip evenly and cut into 12cm lengths; hook one end of each strip over to form a cane. Place on greased tray until candy hardens. Tie a bow onto each cane.

Left: Mixed Fruit Chutney; right: Chilli Apple Chutney

Table and saucepan: Appley Hoare Antiques; teatowels: Accoutrement

PICKLES, CHUTNEYS & RELISHES

Here is a great selection of pickles, chutneys and relishes to give as gifts or to donate to fetes and stalls. Relishes do not keep for more than a couple of months; always store them covered in the refrigerator. Pickles and chutneys will keep well from one season to the next if the jars have been carefully sterilised and sealed, then stored correctly. Jars and non-metal lids will be sterilised if washed in a dishwasher. Fill jars while they are still hot, to the top of the jar, cover loosely, seal jars when cold. Once jars have been opened, store in the refrigerator. Always use a

good quality vinegar for preserving and make sure the fruit and vegetables are firm and unblemished.

Most pickles and chutneys can be cooked in the microwave oven, but the quantities in these recipes will need to be reduced to a manageable proportion. Remember, there is hardly any evaporation in the microwave oven, so recipes might need a little more thickening than recipes cooked in the conventional way.

Pickles and chutneys should be simmered until they are the consistency you desire. Test a spoonful on a

saucer and allow it to become cold before deciding if the recipe is as thick as desired. Use a large saucepan or boiler for cooking pickles and chutneys. Stir occasionally towards the end of the cooking time to make sure the ingredients are not sticking to the base of the saucepan.

MIXED FRUIT CHUTNEY

We used Granny Smith apples in this recipe. This recipe is unsuitable to freeze or microwave.

125g (¾ cup) dried apricots, chopped
125g (¾ cup) dates, chopped
4 large apples, chopped
2 large onions, chopped
1 teaspoon grated fresh ginger
2 teaspoons coarse cooking salt
1 cup brown sugar, firmly packed
2½ cups brown vinegar
1 teaspoon whole cloves
1 teaspoon whole black peppercorns

Place apricots in bowl, cover with hot water, stand 30 minutes. Drain apricots, combine in large saucepan with dates, apples, onions, ginger, salt, sugar and vinegar. Tie cloves and peppercorns in small cloth bag, add to saucepan. Stir constantly over heat, without boiling, until sugar is dissolved. Bring to the boil, reduce heat, simmer uncovered for about 45 minutes or until chutney is thick. Discard cloth bag. Pour into hot sterilised jars; seal when cold.

Makes about 5 cups.

CHILLI APPLE CHUTNEY

We used Granny Smith apples in this recipe. This recipe is not suitable to freeze or microwave.

2 fresh chillies
2kg (about 8) apples, chopped
1 clove garlic, crushed
375g (2¼ cups) raisins, chopped
125g (½ cup) glacé ginger, chopped
1kg (4cups) brown sugar, firmly packed
1 litre (4 cups) white vinegar
1 tablespoon coarse cooking salt
1 tablespoon mixed spice
2 teaspoons five spice powder
1 tablespoon turmeric
2 bay leaves

Seed and chop chillies. Combine all the ingredients in large saucepan. Stir constantly over heat without boiling, until sugar is dissolved. Bring to the boil, reduce heat and simmer uncovered for about 2 hours or until the chutney is thick. Remove bay leaves and pour into hot sterilised jars; seal when cold.

Makes about 7 cups.

PICKLED PEPPERS

Store covered in refrigerator for 3 weeks before using. This recipe is not suitable to freeze or microwave.

2 large onions
3 green peppers, sliced
3 red peppers, sliced
2 tablespoons coarse cooking salt
2 cloves garlic, chopped
bay leaves
1½ cups white vinegar
1 teaspoon yellow mustard seeds
1 teaspoon celery seeds
1 teaspoon whole black peppercorns
¾ cup sugar

Cut onions the same as peppers. Combine onions, peppers and salt in large bowl, cover; stand overnight.

Next day, rinse vegetables under cold water, drain, pack firmly into sterilised jars with a few pieces of garlic and a bay leaf in each jar. Combine remaining ingredients in saucepan, stir constantly over heat until sugar is dissolved, bring to the boil, reduce heat and simmer uncovered 3 minutes. Pour hot vinegar mixture over vegetables; seal while hot.

SPICY PICKLED ONIONS

Use a good quality white malt vinegar for this recipe. Onions are ready to eat after a few days, but they benefit in flavour from 3 to 4 weeks of standing. If you like chillies added for heat and colour, trim the ends from small chillies, leave them whole, then add to saucepan. Whole, unpeeled cloves of garlic

Above: Pickled Peppers; left: Spicy Pickled Onions

can be added, place 3 or 4 in each jar. This recipe is unsuitable to freeze or microwave.

2kg small pickling onions
750g coarse cooking salt
1¼ litres (5 cups) white vinegar
1 tablespoon coarse cooking salt, extra
1 tablespoon sugar
1½ teaspoons whole cloves
2 teaspoons whole allspice (pimento)
2 teaspoons whole black peppercorns

Place unpeeled onions and the 750g salt in a large bowl, add enough water to just float the onions, cover, stand 2 days, stirring occasionally.

Drain liquid from onions. Peel onions carefully leaving ends intact so the onions do not fall apart during the pickling process.

Place onions in heatproof bowl. Cover with boiling water, stand 3 minutes, drain. Repeat this process twice. After draining the onions well for the third time, place them into hot sterilised jars.

Combine the remaining ingredients in saucepan. Bring to the boil, reduce heat, simmer uncovered for 15 minutes, pour into jars over onions; seal while hot.

GINGER MANGO CHUTNEY

This recipe is unsuitable to freeze or microwave.

4kg (about 12) firm under-ripe mangoes, chopped
310g (2 cups) raisins or sultanas
2 tablespoons grated fresh ginger
2 teaspoons coarse cooking salt
4 cloves garlic, crushed
1 fresh chilli, finely chopped
1½ cups brown vinegar
1¼kg (5 cups) sugar

Combine all ingredients in large saucepan, stir constantly over heat, without boiling, until sugar is dissolved. Bring to the boil, reduce heat, cover, simmer 10 minutes. Remove lid, simmer for about 20 minutes or until thick. Pour into hot sterilised jars; seal when cold.

Makes about 6 cups.

CAULIFLOWER TOMATO PICKLE

This recipe is unsuitable to freeze or microwave.

1 small cauliflower
750g (about 6) tomatoes
1 cucumber
4 onions, chopped
1 cup coarse cooking salt
2 cups white vinegar
1¼ cups brown sugar, firmly packed

Ginger Mango Chutney

1 tablespoon yellow mustard seeds
1 teaspoon dry mustard
1 teaspoon ground ginger
½ teaspoon turmeric

Cut cauliflower into flowerets, cut tomatoes into eighths, remove seeds from cucumber, cut cucumber into strips. Layer all the vegetables in a large bowl, sprinkling each layer with salt, cover vegetables with water; cover bowl, stand overnight.

Next day, drain and rinse the vegetables. Place vegetables in large saucepan, add vinegar, sugar and remaining ingredients. Stir constantly over heat, without boiling, until the sugar is dissolved. Bring to the boil, reduce heat and simmer uncovered, for about 10 minutes or until vegetables are just tender. Remove from heat. Use a slotted spoon to transfer the vegetables to hot sterilised jars, pour in enough hot cooking liquid to fill jars; seal when cold.

Makes about 4 cups.

BEAN RELISH

Store this relish in the refrigerator; it will keep for about a month. This recipe is unsuitable to freeze.

310g can butter beans
190g can champignons
375ml can V8 vegetable juice
1 stick celery, chopped
1 onion, chopped
1½ tablespoons cornflour
1 teaspoon sugar
¼ cup French dressing
few drops tabasco
1 tablespoon chopped parsley

Drain and rinse beans, drain. Rinse and halve champignons, combine with beans and vegetable juice in saucepan. Add celery and onion. Blend cornflour and sugar with dressing, stir into bean mixture, stir constantly over heat until mixture boils and thickens, reduce heat, simmer 1 minute (or microwave on HIGH for about 2 minutes). Add tabasco and parsley, pour into hot

Bowls: Artiana Imports; table: Appley Hoare Antiques

Clockwise from left: Mustard Pickles; Cauliflower Tomato Pickle; Bean Relish; Corn Pepper Relish; Ripe Tomato Chutney

79

Sweet Beetroot Chutney

sterilised jars; seal when cold.
Makes about 3 cups.

SWEET BEETROOT CHUTNEY

We used Granny Smith apples in this recipe. This recipe is unsuitable to freeze or microwave.

1kg beetroot
1 cup sugar
1 onion, finely chopped
2 cups white vinegar
3 large apples, chopped

Cut stems and leaves from beetroot, do not break skin of beetroot. Place beetroot in large saucepan, cover with water. Bring to the boil covered, reduce heat, simmer for about 1 hour or until beetroot are tender. Cool slightly before peeling and chopping.

Combine sugar, onion and vinegar in large saucepan, stir over heat, without boiling, until sugar is dissolved. Bring to the boil, add apples, simmer uncovered for about 15 minutes or until thick. Add beetroot, simmer fur-

ther 5 minutes. Pour into hot sterilised jars; seal when cold.
Makes about 4 cups.

RIPE TOMATO CHUTNEY

We used Granny Smith apples in this recipe. This recipe is not suitable to freeze or microwave.

2kg (about 8) tomatoes, peeled, chopped
3 large onions, chopped
3 large apples, chopped
3 sticks celery, chopped
155g (1 cup) sultanas
1¾ cups brown vinegar
2½ cups brown sugar, firmly packed
1 tablespoon curry powder
1 tablespoon ground ginger
1 tablespoon dry mustard
1 teaspoon ground cinnamon
2 tablespoons coarse cooking salt

Combine tomatoes, onions, apples, celery and sultanas in large saucepan with vinegar, sugar, spices and salt. Stir constantly over heat, without boiling, until sugar is dissolved. Bring to the boil, reduce heat, simmer uncovered for about 2 hours or until chutney

is thick. Pour into hot sterilised jars; seal when cold.
Makes about 9 cups.

CORN PEPPER RELISH

Store relish in the refrigerator for up to 2 weeks. This recipe is unsuitable to freeze.

1 cup white vinegar
⅓ cup sugar
½ teaspoon coarse cooking salt
½ teaspoon turmeric
2 sticks celery, chopped
2 red peppers, chopped
2 x 310g cans corn kernels, drained
1 tablespoon cornflour
2 tablespoons water

Combine vinegar, sugar, salt and turmeric in saucepan, stir over low heat, without boiling, until sugar is dissolved. Add celery and peppers. Bring to the boil, reduce heat, simmer uncovered for 10 minutes, add corn. Blend cornflour with water, stir into corn mixture, stir until mixture boils and thickens (or microwave on HIGH for about 5 minutes). Pour into hot sterilised jars; seal when cold.
Makes about 4 cups.

MUSTARD PICKLES

This recipe is unsuitable to freeze or microwave.

½ small cabbage, shredded
3 onions, sliced
2 green peppers, chopped
2 red peppers, chopped
¼ cup coarse cooking salt
2 cups white vinegar
1 cup brown sugar, lightly packed
2 cups white sugar
2 teaspoons dry mustard
1 teaspoon turmeric
1 teaspoon ground ginger
¼ cup plain flour
½ cup water
1 tablespoon yellow mustard seeds
1 tablespoon celery seeds

Combine cabbage, onions, peppers and salt in large bowl; mix well, cover, stand overnight.

Drain vegetables, rinse well under cold water; drain. Combine vinegar and sugars in large saucepan, stir over heat, without boiling, until sugar is dissolved. Bring to the boil, add vegetables, reduce heat, simmer uncovered for 5 minutes. Blend mustard, turmeric, ginger and flour with the water, stir into vegetable mixture, stir constantly over heat until mixture boils and thickens, reduce heat, simmer 10 minutes. Add seeds, pour into hot sterilised jars; seal when cold.
Makes about 8 cups.

Individual Boiled Fruit Cakes and Puddings

CAKES

INDIVIDUAL BOILED FRUIT CAKES AND PUDDINGS

Use any type sherry, rum, brandy or whisky in this recipe. The cakes and puddings (in their containers) will freeze for about 2 months. This recipe is not suitable to microwave.

2kg mixed fruit, chopped
250g butter
1½ cups brown sugar, firmly packed
⅓ cup golden syrup
2 cups sherry
4 eggs, lightly beaten
2 cups self-raising flour

2 cups plain flour
2 teaspoons mixed spice

Combine the fruit, butter, sugar, golden syrup and half the sherry in a large saucepan. Bring to the boil stirring, reduce heat, cover, simmer 5 minutes; cool to room temperature. Stir in the remaining sherry, eggs and sifted dry ingredients.

To make the cakes: Half fill well-greased nut-roll tins (9cm x 18cm). Mixture will make 5 cakes. Bake in moderately slow oven for about 1½ hours, cool in tins.

To make the puddings: Use dish washer-proof plastic containers with screw-top lids (as shown in picture). These are available from large department, hardware and chain stores.

Fill containers (no need to grease) to within 2cm of the top with mixture, screw lids on firmly. Place containers on wire rack in boiler, add enough boiling water to come half-way up sides of plastic containers. If the boiler is large enough, several of these puddings can be cooked at the one time.

Mixture will make 6 puddings. Boil for 2½ hours; reboil 1 hour on day of serving if pudding is to be served hot.

HONEY FRUIT SLICE

This rich, fruity slice should be served in small pieces. The cake will keep in an airtight container for about 3 months; it will also freeze for the same period of time. This recipe is not suitable to microwave.

500g (3¼ cups) mixed fruit, chopped
125g (½ cup) chopped dried plums
(prunes)
125g (½ cup) chopped glacé figs
125g (½ cup) chopped glacé
apricots
125g (1 cup) chopped pecans or
walnuts
3 eggs, lightly beaten
⅓ cup honey
1¼ cups plain flour

Combine fruit and nuts in large bowl with eggs, honey and sifted flour, mix well. Press mixture evenly into greased and greased paper-lined 25cm x 30cm Swiss roll pan. Bake in slow oven for 1 hour. Cool in pan, cut when cold.

ABOVE: Honey Fruit Slice

ABOVE: Ground Almond Fruit Cake
LEFT: Apple Cakes

APPLE CAKES

Aluminium foil pie dishes are available from most supermarkets or hardware stores. Stew 3 Granny Smith apples, allow to cool and drain well. These cakes can be cooked a day before required. This recipe is not suitable to freeze or microwave.

1½ cups self-raising flour
¾ cup castor sugar
2 tablespoons full-cream powdered
milk
125g butter
1 tablespoon water
1 egg

¼ cup water, extra
½ teaspoon ground cinnamon
425g can pie apples
icing sugar

Sift flour, sugar and milk powder into bowl, rub in butter. (This can be done in a food processor.) Divide mixture in half, add 1 tablespoon water to half, mix to a firm dough. Divide dough into 3, press each piece over base of 3 x 15cm aluminium foil pie dishes. Spread one-third of the apples into each dish. Place remaining flour mixture into small bowl of electric mixer. Add egg, extra water and cinnamon, beat on low speed until ingredients are combined. Increase speed to medium, beat until mixture is smooth. Divide mixture over apples, spread evenly. Bake in moder-ate oven for about 30 minutes. Sprinkle with sifted icing sugar when cold.

Makes 3.

GROUND ALMOND FRUIT CAKE

An ideal Christmas cake for those people who can't tolerate gluten (which comes from flour) in their diet. The cakes keep well in the refrigerator or freezer, if sealed tightly, for up to 3 months. This recipe is not suitable to microwave.

250g (1 cup) seedless dates
150g (⅔ cup) mixed peel
90g (½ cup) red glacé cherries
90g (½ cup) green glacé cherries
80g (½ cup) raisins
250g (1½ cups) brazil nuts
185g (1½ cups) pecans or walnuts
100g (¾ cup) packaged ground almonds
½ teaspoon baking powder
3 eggs
2 tablespoons honey
1 teaspoon vanilla essence
2 tablespoons rum

Place whole fruit and nuts in bowl, then stir in ground almonds and baking powder. Beat eggs in small bowl with electric mixer until thick and creamy, beat in honey and essence; stir into the fruit mixture.

Spread evenly into 2 greased and paper-lined 8cm x 26cm bar pans. Bake in slow oven for 1½ to 2 hours or until firm. Brush hot cakes with rum, wrap in foil, cool in pans overnight.

Festive Fruit and Nut Bread

FESTIVE FRUIT AND NUT BREAD

Serve the bread sliced thinly and buttered. Kirsch is a cherry-flavoured liqueur. Amaretto (an almond-flavoured liqueur) or brandy can also be used. Bread can be baked up to a day before serving. It will freeze for up to 2 months. This recipe is not suitable to microwave.

250g (1½ cups) chopped raisins
250g (1½ cups) sultanas
125g (¾ cup) currants
125g (½ cup) mixed peel
125g (⅔ cup) quartered glacé
   cherries
¼ cup Kirsch
250g (2 cups) slivered almonds
2 x 7g packets dry yeast
1 cup hot water
1 teaspoon sugar
5 cups plain flour
2 tablespoons sugar, extra
1 teaspoon mixed spice
2 eggs, lightly beaten
60g butter, melted
GLAZE
1 cup icing sugar
1 teaspoon soft butter
2 tablespoons water, approximately

Combine raisins, sultanas, currants, peel, cherries and Kirsch in bowl, cover, stand overnight.

Next day, stir in almonds. Combine the dry yeast, water and sugar in bowl, cover, stand in warm place for about 5 minutes or until frothy. Sift flour, extra sugar and spice into large bowl, make well in centre, stir in yeast mixture, eggs and butter. Turn onto lightly floured surface, knead about 10 minutes, or until smooth. Return dough to lightly greased bowl, cover with plastic wrap, stand in warm place for about 1 hour or until dough is doubled in bulk.

Knead in combined almonds and fruit mixture in several batches. Divide dough in half, divide each half into 3 equal portions, shape each portion into a 40cm rope. Plait the "ropes" together, place each plait onto lightly greased oven trays, cover loosely with plastic wrap, stand in warm place for about 30 minutes or until dough is risen. Bake in moderate oven for about 35 minutes or until bread sounds hollow when tapped. Brush with glaze while hot.

Glaze: Place sifted icing sugar into small bowl, stir in butter and enough water to give a thick consistency.

EXTRAS

This curry powder and paste will give an authentic taste to chicken, fish, meat and vegetable curries. Include a note with a gift like this, to tell the recipient how much of the powder or paste to use.

The powder and paste are at their best if used as soon as they are made; however, they do store quite well in the refrigerator in an airtight container for several months.

Both of these recipes will give you a spicy, slightly hot curry; if more heat is preferred, add or increase chilli powder as you are making it, or even when you start to use the powder or paste. This recipe is unsuitable to freeze or microwave.

CURRY POWDER

You will need to use about 3 teaspoons of powder to each 500g meat.

¼ cup coriander seeds
2 tablespoons caraway seeds
2 tablespoons turmeric
1½ tablespoons cumin seeds
1½ tablespoons whole black
   peppercorns
½ teaspoon cardamom seeds
½ teaspoon fenugreek
1 tablespoon ground cinnamon
2 tablespoons ground ginger
½ teaspoon whole cloves
pinch nutmeg

Blend all ingredients until finely ground. Store in airtight container.
   Makes about ¾ cup.

CURRY PASTE

You will need to use about 2 tablespoons of paste to each 500g meat.

2 tablespoons ground coriander
1 tablespoon ground cinnamon
1 tablespoon dry mustard
¼ teaspoon chilli powder
1 tablespoon turmeric
1 tablespoon ground ginger

Tiles, plate and jar: Country Floors, Sydney.

2 teaspoons sugar
1 clove garlic, crushed
½ cup oil
1 tablespoon lemon juice
2 tablespoons vinegar
Combine dry ingredients in a saucepan. Gradually stir in combined garlic, oil, lemon juice and vinegar, mix to a smooth paste. Stir constantly over a low heat for a few minutes or until slightly thickened; cool mixture to room temperature before placing into jars; seal securely.

Makes about 1 cup.

Front: Curry Paste; back: ingredients for Curry Powder

85

Glass bowls: Wedgwood; table: Appley Hoare Antiques; salt and pepper grinder: Accoutrement.

ABOVE: Almond Pecan Praline
LEFT: Salt and Pepper Surprise

Combine all ingredients, store in airtight container. Makes about 2 cups.

Three Peppers

Use equal quantities of whole dried green, black and white peppercorns.

ALMOND PECAN PRALINE

Praline is a handy gift, it is also simple to make and tastes great when used as a decoration for cakes and desserts, or as a topping for ice-cream. Praline can be chopped roughly into large pieces or crushed finely; stored in an airtight container at room temperature it will keep indefinitely.

250g (1½ cups) blanched almonds
125g (1 cup) pecans
3 cups castor sugar

Toast almonds and pecans on oven tray in moderate oven for about 5 minutes, cool. Place nuts on oiled tray.

Sprinkle sugar over base of large heavy-based frying pan, cook over medium heat, without stirring, until sugar begins to melt. Gently and slowly stir sugar until completely melted and golden brown. Pour toffee over nuts, stand at room temperature until set, chop coarsely with knife or crush in processor until fine.

SALT AND PEPPER SURPRISE

Choose attractive see-through salt and pepper grinders and fill with this wonderful salt and pepper combination to create an unusual gift.

500g packet rock salt
3 teaspoons paprika

2 teaspoons dry mustard
2 teaspoons dried basil leaves
2 teaspoons dried oregano leaves
1 teaspoon dried marjoram leaves
1 teaspoon dried thyme leaves
1 teaspoon garlic powder
1 teaspoon curry powder
½ teaspoon onion powder

·SWEET· DELIGHTS

A tantalising array to add the perfect finishing touch to a meal, or to make an afternoon celebration especially sweet. Accompany them with richly-flavoured coffee, aromatic tea or chilled champagne.

Florentines

SWEET DELIGHTS

FLORENTINES

Florentines are easy to make with a little practice. The trick is to make a few first to establish the cooking time and colour and to gain a little confidence in handling the biscuit. The time given is a guide only, it depends mainly on the accuracy of the oven. Once you've mastered the biscuits, then cook 2 trays at a time, staggering the times you place them in the oven.

The best way of cooking the biscuits is to put a tray in the top position, then after 4 minutes change it to a lower shelf, and put another tray in the top position. This way the biscuits will brown evenly.

As a general rule, biscuits cook well in the lower half to the centre of an electric oven and from the centre to the upper half in a gas oven. Work out the shelf position before turning the oven on. Follow the manufacturers' instructions for the best cooking results. This recipe is not suitable to freeze or microwave.

60g butter
⅓ cup brown sugar
2 tablespoons plain flour
¼ cup finely chopped walnuts
¼ cup finely chopped flaked almonds
1 tablespoon finely chopped mixed peel
⅓ cup finely chopped glacé cherries
250g dark chocolate

1 Cream butter, sugar and flour in small bowl with electric mixer until light and fluffy. Stir nuts and fruit into creamed mixture.

2 Place heaped teaspoonfuls of mixture onto a lightly greased oven

tray, allow about 8cm for spreading. Flatten gently into circles with fingertips. Bake in moderate oven for about 8 minutes or until mixture is bubbly and golden brown.

3 Remove from oven, use spatula to make rough edges smooth.

4 Slide spatula under soft biscuits very gently to lift from tray. When biscuits feel firm enough to handle without breaking, lift onto wire racks to cool. Repeat with more mixture.

5 Melt chocolate in bowl over hot water, cool until slightly thickened. Spread base of biscuits with chocolate. When almost set, run fork through chocolate to give a wavy effect. Allow to set at room temperature; if weather is hot, set in refrigerator.
Makes about 24.

THE TRUFFLE TREE

The "tree" is a delightful, help-yourself centrepiece for the Christmas table with melt-in-the-mouth truffles; the "tree" holds about 45 truffles, they can be all the same variety or an assortment. Polystyrene balls are available from craft shops. All the truffles will keep well in the refrigerator for up to a month. The truffles are not suitable to freeze or microwave.

18cm diameter terracotta flower pot
30cm piece wooden dowelling
1 polystyrene ball
gold paint
Christmas decorations
toothpicks

Glue piece of dowelling into hole in centre of flower pot base, paint pot and dowelling with gold paint, stand until completely dry.

Arrange Christmas decorations inside pot, gently push polystyrene ball onto top of dowelling. Push toothpicks into polystyrene ball at regular intervals, about 2cm apart; push truffles gently onto toothpicks, as pictured. Keep tree refrigerated until required.

CHERRY BRANDY TRUFFLES

60g dark chocolate, chopped
125g (¾ cup) blanched almonds
60g butter
1 egg yolk
125g packaged plain sweet biscuits
¼ cup finely chopped glacé pineapple
2 tablespoons finely chopped glacé apricots
2 tablespoons finely chopped glacé cherries
2 tablespoons Cherry Brandy

Melt chocolate over hot water, cool slightly. Toast almonds on oven tray, in moderate oven for about 5 minutes; cool, chop finely.

Beat butter in small bowl until light and creamy, beat in egg yolk. Stir in cooled chocolate, ¼ cup of the almonds, finely crushed biscuits, pineapple, apricots, cherries and Cherry Brandy, mix well. Roll tablespoons of mixture into balls, toss in remaining almonds, cover, refrigerate.

Makes about 25.

COFFEE LIQUEUR TRUFFLES

Tia Maria and Kahlua are coffee-flavoured liqueurs.

90g (½ cup) sultanas
90g (¼ cup) finely chopped raisins
½ cup finely chopped glace cherries
2 tablespoons Tia Maria or Kahlua
60g (½ cup) finely chopped roasted hazelnuts
250g packet cream cheese, softened
¼ cup icing sugar
125g dark chocolate
coconut

Combine sultanas, raisins, cherries in bowl, stir in liqueur, nuts, cream cheese and sifted icing sugar. Melt chocolate over hot water, stir into cream cheese, cover, refrigerate 1 hour. Roll tablespoons of mixture into balls, toss in coconut, cover, refrigerate.

Makes about 30.

CHESTNUT RUM TRUFFLES

125g dark chocolate, chopped
60g butter
½ cup unsweetened chestnut purée
2¾ cups plain cake crumbs
½ cup icing sugar
1 tablespoon rum
chocolate sprinkles

Melt chocolate and butter over hot water. Combine chocolate mixture with chestnut purée, cake crumbs, sifted icing sugar and rum in bowl, mix well, cover, refrigerate several hours. Roll tablespoons of mixture into balls, toss in sprinkles, cover, refrigerate.

Makes about 20.

WHITE CHRISTMAS TRUFFLES

250g (1 cup) finely chopped mixed glacé fruit
2 tablespoons brandy
3 x 100g blocks white chocolate, chopped
15g butter
½ cup icing sugar
185g (1½ cups) finely chopped walnuts

Combine fruit with brandy in bowl, cover, stand overnight. Melt chocolate and butter over hot water, add chocolate mixture and sifted icing sugar to fruit mixture, mix well, press mixture together with hands. Roll tablespoons

The Truffle Tree

89

of mixture into balls, toss in walnuts, cover, refrigerate.

Makes about 20.

ALMOND TRUFFLES

Amaretto is an almond-flavoured liqueur; brandy can be substituted.

90g (1 cup) flaked almonds
185g dark chocolate, chopped
⅓ cup thickened cream
250g (2 cups) packaged ground almonds
1 cup icing sugar
1 egg white
1 tablespoon Amaretto

Toast flaked almonds on oven tray in moderate oven for about 5 minutes, cool. Melt chocolate over hot water, stir in cream, ground almonds, sifted icing sugar, unbeaten egg white and liqueur. Press mixture together with hand, roll tablespoons of mixture into balls, toss balls in flaked almonds; cover, refrigerate.

Makes about 20.

ORANGE TRUFFLES

Cointreau and Grand Marnier are citrus-flavoured liqueurs.

200g dark chocolate, chopped
60g butter
1 teaspoon grated orange rind
2 tablespoons icing sugar
1 tablespoon finely chopped mixed peel
1 tablespoon Cointreau or Grand Marnier
cocoa

Melt chocolate and butter in bowl over hot water. Stir in rind, sifted icing sugar, peel and liqueur; cover, refrigerate several hours. Roll tablespoons of mixture into balls, toss in cocoa, cover, refrigerate.

Makes about 25.

CARAMEL NUT TARTLETS

We used small, square, fluted tins to make these tartlets; shallow patty pans can be substituted (this quantity will make about 12). Pastry cases can be baked up to 4 days ahead and stored in an airtight container, then filled with caramel nut mixture the day before they are required. This recipe is not suitable to freeze or microwave.

PASTRY
¾ cup plain flour
1 tablespoon custard powder
1 tablespoon icing sugar
60g butter
2 teaspoons water, approximately
FILLING
¼ cup blanched almonds
¼ cup hazelnuts
¼ cup pecans or walnuts
¼ cup sugar
2 teaspoons liquid glucose
2 teaspoons water
2 tablespoons cream

Pastry: Sift dry ingredients into bowl, rub in butter, add enough water to make ingredients cling together. Knead gently on lightly floured surface until smooth, cover, refrigerate 30 minutes. Roll pastry between pieces of plastic wrap, until about 2mm thick. Cut pastry into 5cm rounds, press into tins, pierce bases well with fork. Bake pastry cases in moderately hot oven for about 10 minutes or until pastry is lightly browned. Cool in tins.

Filling: Chop nuts evenly, toast on oven tray in moderate oven for about 5 minutes. Combine sugar, glucose and water in small saucepan, stir constantly over heat, without boiling, until sugar is dissolved. Boil rapidly, without stirring, for about 3 minutes or until sugar mixture has turned golden brown. Stir in cream and nuts, spoon mixture into pastry cases while hot.

Makes about 24.

Caramel Nut Tartlets

APRICOT TOFFEE PUFFS

Puffs can be cooked up to a week before required and stored in an airtight container; they can be frozen for 2 months. Apricot cream can be made up to 2 days ahead, covered and refrigerated. The puffs can be completed up to 6 hours before serving. Store in a cool, dry place. This recipe is not suitable to microwave.

CHOUX PASTRY
½ cup water
30g butter
½ cup plain flour
2 eggs, lightly beaten
APRICOT CREAM
100g (½ cup) chopped dried apricots
¼ cup brandy
¼ cup water
60g packaged cream cheese
½ cup sour cream
2 tablespoons castor sugar
TOFFEE
1 cup sugar
⅓ cup water
1 tablespoon brown vinegar

Choux Pastry: Place water and butter in saucepan bring to the boil; immediately stir in flour all at once. Stir vigorously over heat until mixture leaves sides of pan and forms a smooth ball. Remove from heat, stand 3 minutes. Place into processor or small bowl of electric mixer, gradually beat in eggs. Spoon mixture into piping bag fitted with a 1cm plain tube. Pipe small mounds (about 2 teaspoonfuls) onto lightly greased oven trays about 3cm apart. Bake in hot oven 10 minutes, reduce heat to moderate, bake further 15 minutes or until golden brown and crisp. Remove from oven, cut a small round from base of each puff; reserve rounds. When puffs are cold, pipe apricot cream into puffs, replace reserved rounds. Carefully drizzle toffee over the puffs.

Apricot Cream: Combine apricots, brandy and water in saucepan, bring to the boil, reduce heat, simmer 5 minutes, or until liquid has been absorbed, cool to room temperature.

Puree mixture in blender processor until smooth. Add cream cheese, sour cream and sugar, blend until smooth. Spoon mixture into piping bag fitted with plain tube.

Toffee: Combine sugar, water and vinegar in saucepan, stir constantly over heat, without boiling, until sugar is dissolved. Bring to the boil, boil rapidly, uncovered, without stirring, for about 5 minutes or until toffee is golden brown and a teaspoon of toffee will crack when dropped into a cup of cold water. Stand toffee for about 5 minutes, or until thickened slightly, before using.

RICH CHOCOLATE-FILLED RUSSES

Chocolate filling can be made and kept unrefrigerated in a cool place up to 4 hours ahead. Pipe filling into cigarette russes just before serving; cigarette russes are available from specialty food shops. If unavailable, the filling can be piped onto small shortbread biscuits. This recipe is not suitable to freeze or microwave.

100g dark chocolate, chopped
100g milk chocolate, chopped
¼ cup dark rum
250g unsalted butter, softened
¼ cup icing sugar
2 eggs, separated
90g (¾ cup) packaged ground almonds
150g packet cigarette russes

Melt chocolates and rum over hot water, cool, do not allow to set.

Beat butter and sifted icing sugar in small bowl with electric mixer until

ABOVE: from left: Apricot Toffee Puffs, Rich Chocolate-Filled Russes
LEFT: Chocolate Cherry Rounds

creamy, stir in egg yolks and almonds, then chocolate. Beat egg whites until soft peaks form, fold into chocolate mixture. Spoon into piping bag fitted with a small fluted tube, pipe into cigarette russes, serve immediately.

Makes about 18.

CHOCOLATE CHERRY ROUNDS

These will keep well in the refrigerator for at least a month. This recipe is not suitable to freeze or microwave.

125g butter
2 cups icing sugar
¼ cup thickened cream
1 teaspoon rum
2 cups coconut
pink food colouring
185g dark chocolate
Melt butter in saucepan until it is a deep golden brown, remove from heat. Stir in sifted icing sugar, cream, rum and coconut. Tint with pink colouring. Roll teaspoonfuls of mixture into balls, place on tray. Melt chocolate over hot

water. Place toothpick into each ball, dip balls in chocolate. Place on foil-covered tray, refrigerate until firm.

Makes about 35.

BRANDIED CHOCOLATE DROPS

These can be stored, covered, in the refrigerator for up to 2 weeks. This recipe is not suitable to freeze or microwave.

250g dark chocolate, chopped
½ cup thickened cream
2 teaspoons brandy
3 tablespoons cocoa
1 tablespoon icing sugar
Melt chocolate and cream in saucepan without boiling, cool to room temperature. Stir in brandy, refrigerate until firm, then beat with whisk or electric mixer until light in colour. Drop teaspoonfuls of mixture into combined sifted cocoa and icing sugar, roll quickly into balls. Place balls in foil containers, refrigerate until firm.

Makes about 30.

Back: Chocolate Almond Macaroons; front: Brandied Chocolate Drops

CHOCOLATE ALMOND MACAROONS

Macaroons will keep well in an airtight container for 2 weeks; they can be frozen for 2 months. This recipe is not suitable to microwave.

2 eggs, separated
¾ cup castor sugar
2 tablespoons cocoa
250g (2¾) cups coconut
¼ cup packaged ground almonds
Beat egg whites in small bowl with electric mixer until soft peaks form. Beat in egg yolks, gradually beat in sugar and sifted cocoa, beat until sugar is dissolved. Stir in combined coconut and almonds. Drop tablespoonfuls of mixture onto lightly greased oven trays. Bake in moderately slow oven for about 15 minutes or until lightly browned.

Makes about 40.

Delectable
EASTER
Delectable ... • Details •

*Easter traditionally means hot
cross buns straight from the oven,
deliciously sweet helpings of
chocolate and much indulgence.
We have chosen recipes which will
help the holiday pass sweetly!*

Easy Crayon Easter Eggs

EASY CRAYON EASTER EGGS

This is a good idea for children who want to design their own eggs for the family. The method is simple but effective. Tell the children to crayon lightly on the delicate shells.

Use different coloured crayons to draw patterns over hard-boiled eggs. Tint bowls of water with various food colourings, immerse eggs, stand five minutes; drain well. Pat shells dry with absorbent paper.

HOT CROSS BUNS

To freeze buns: When buns are cold (do not glaze) wrap in foil, freeze for up to 1 month. Place frozen foil-wrapped buns in moderate oven, bake about 45 minutes, brush tops with glaze. Or, place unbaked buns in pan. Cover with plastic food wrap, wrap tightly in foil, freeze for up to 2 weeks. Remove wrapping, thaw buns at room temperature, allow to rise. Pipe with crosses, bake and glaze. This recipe is not suitable to microwave.

30g compressed yeast
¼ cup sugar
4 cups plain flour
1½ cups milk
1 teaspoon salt
½ teaspoon mixed spice
½ teaspoon ground cinnamon
60g butter
1 egg, lightly beaten
90g (½ cup) sultanas
FLOUR PASTE FOR CROSSES
½ cup plain flour
2 teaspoons sugar
⅓ cup water, approximately
GLAZE
1 tablespoon sugar
1 teaspoon gelatine
1 tablespoon hot water

Cream yeast in a small bowl with 1 teaspoon each of the sugar and flour, add warm milk, mix well. Cover, stand in warm place for about 15 minutes or until mixture is frothy.

Sift flour, salt, sugar and spices into large bowl. Rub in butter, add egg, sultanas and yeast mixture, beat well with wooden spoon. Cover bowl with clean cloth, stand in warm place for about 40 minutes or until dough is doubled in bulk. Punch dough down, turn onto floured surface, knead well for about 5 minutes or until the dough is smooth and elastic.

Cut dough into 16 pieces, knead each piece into a round shape. Put buns in lightly greased 23cm square slab pan, stand in warm place for about 15 minutes or until buns reach the top edge of the pan. Place flour paste for crosses in piping bag fitted with small

Hot Cross Buns

plain tube and pipe crosses on buns. Bake in hot oven 20 minutes. Brush tops with hot glaze while buns are still hot from the oven.

Flour paste for crosses: Use a teaspoon to blend flour and sugar in cup with enough water to give a smooth paste, stir until free from lumps.

Glaze: Combine all ingredients in small saucepan, stir constantly over heat, without boiling, until sugar and gelatine are dissolved.

MARZIPAN EASTER EGGS

Try this recipe made into tiny eggs to serve with coffee. This recipe is not suitable to freeze or microwave.

250g blanched almonds
⅔ cup sugar
2 tablespoons water
1 tablespoon lemon juice
1 teaspoon brandy
125g dark chocolate
15g Copha

Blend or process almonds until as fine as possible. Combine sugar, water and lemon juice in small saucepan, stir over heat, without boiling, until sugar is dissolved. Increase heat, boil rapidly, without stirring, for 3 minutes or until syrup is thick (it must not be changed in colour). Syrup should form a soft ball of toffee when a teaspoon of syrup is dropped into a cup of gold water.

If a candy thermometer is available, boil until syrup reaches a temperature of 114°C (240°F). Remove from heat immediately, allow bubbles to subside, then pour in a thin, steady stream onto ground almonds.

Mix syrup in fairly quickly, using a fork to mix, then use your hand when mixture becomes too thick to stir. Wrap mixture in plastic wrap or foil, leave until completely cold.

Work brandy into mixture with fingers dusted with icing sugar. Mixture can be stored, wrapped, for several weeks in the refrigerator. Return to room temperature before using.

Divide mixture into five equal portions. Mould into smooth egg shapes with hands, stand on foil-covered tray. Melt chocolate and Copha over hot water; spread a little chocolate mixture over base of each egg, return to tray. Spoon chocolate over egg, let chocolate run onto foil. When chocolate is set, it can be removed, heated gently and used again. If room is cool, leave chocolate to set at room temperature, but if hot, refrigerate until set. If desired, decorate with some remaining chocolate piped from a bag fitted with a small plain tube.

Makes 5 large eggs.

Left: Marzipan Easter Eggs; right: Coconut Easter Eggs

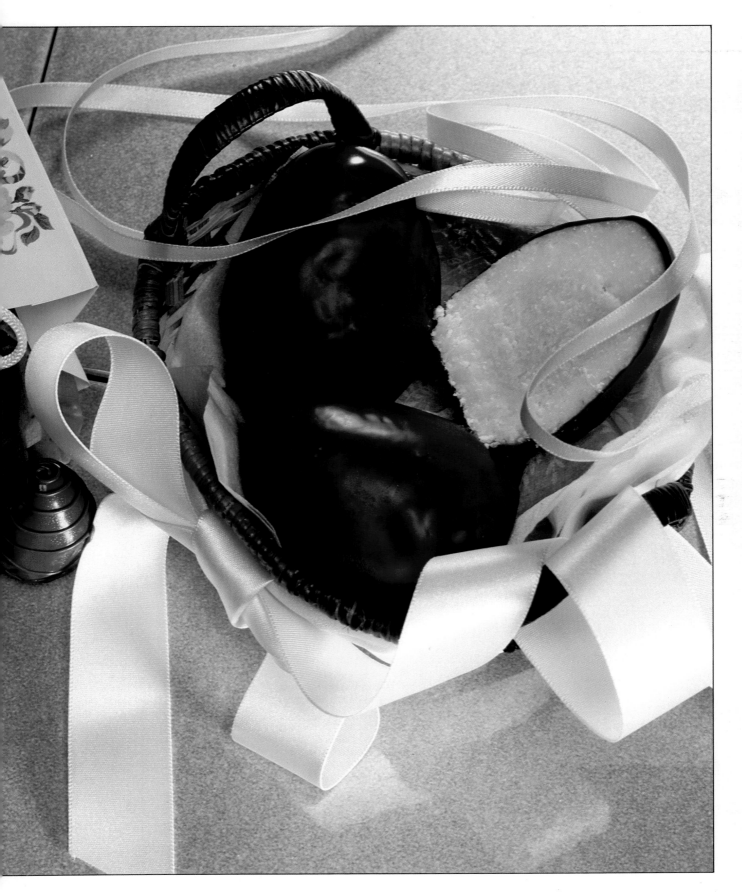

Easter Bunnies

COCONUT EASTER EGGS

Eggs can be made up to 2 weeks ahead of time. This recipe is not suitable to freeze.

45g Copha, chopped
2 cups icing sugar
1 cup coconut
1 egg white
¼ teaspoon coconut essence
yellow food colouring
125g dark chocolate, chopped

Melt Copha in saucepan over low heat. Sift icing sugar into bowl, stir in coconut, Copha, unbeaten egg white and essence, mix well with a fork. Remove ¼ cup of the mixture, tint yellow with colouring. Divide remaining mixture into 5 equal parts (about a heaped tablespoonful for each), roll each white portion into a smooth ball between hands, cut each ball in half, make an indentation with finger.

Divide yellow portion into 5 equal parts, roll into smooth balls. Place an 'egg yolk' into the indentation of each 'egg white'.

Press joins of egg white together gently, then roll between palms of hands until smooth and egg-shaped. Repeat with remaining mixture. Place each egg on foil-covered tray, stand about 30 minutes or until slightly firm to touch.

Melt chocolate in pan over hot water. Coat one egg at a time, spread about ½ teaspoon chocolate underneath each egg, return to tray. Spread tops with chocolate.

Immediately after each egg has been coated, gently push the egg across the foil. This ensures that the base of the eggs are coated and sealed with chocolate and avoids a large pool of chocolate around base. If weather is hot or humid, place eggs in refrigerator until set; if cool, leave to set at room temperature.

Makes 5.

EASTER BUNNIES

Trace around the bunny shapes, using picture as a guide; cut out the bunny

shapes from light cardboard. You will need a small can of evaporated milk and a variety of food colourings to make the bunnies. You'll also need a variety of coloured sweets and Choc bits to decorate the bunnies, and some fine paint brushes to coat them. Undecorated bunnies can be stored in an airtight container for several weeks. This recipe is not suitable to freeze or microwave.

BUNNY BISCUITS
125g butter
1 teaspoon vanilla essence
1 cup castor sugar
1 egg
2 teaspoons milk

1½ cups self-raising flour
1 cup plain flour

Cream butter, essence and sugar in small bowl with electric mixer, beat until light and fluffy, beat in egg and milk. Stir in sifted flours in 3 lots, knead dough on floured surface until dough is firm enough to handle, cover, refrigerate 30 minutes.

Roll out dough on well-floured surface to 5mm thickness, cut out shapes, place shapes onto lightly greased oven trays, about 2cm apart. Bake in moderate oven for about 15 minutes; leave on trays to cool.

Place Choc bits in place for eyes while biscuits are still warm.

To decorate bunnies: Pour about a

tablespoon of evaporated milk onto a saucer, add colouring drop by drop until the colour is as strong as you like; mix colouring well through milk. Mix as many colours as required. Paint rabbits, decorate with sweets.

Ice-cream wafers or cones can be used for ears; it is best to push the cut-out ear shapes gently into the head of the bunny while the biscuit is still hot from the oven. They will sit firmly in position when the biscuits are cold. Sweets need to be attached with a tiny dab of icing. Mix a tablespoon of icing sugar with a few drops of milk to a paste-like consistency, this will dry and hold the sweets on firmly.

Makes 12.

CHOCOLATE ICE-CREAM EGGS

We used plastic egg moulds which measured 9cm long.

CHOCOLATE SHELLS
250g dark compound cooking chocolate
EGG WHITES
300ml carton thickened cream
125g dark chocolate, chopped
2 eggs
2 tablespoons castor sugar
EGG YOLKS
100g white chocolate
2 teaspoons butter
2 teaspoons sifted icing sugar
2 teaspoons brandy
¼ cup roasted hazelnuts, finely chopped

Egg whites: Reserve 2 tablespoons of the cream for "egg yolks", beat remaining cream until soft peaks form. Melt chocolate over hot water, cool. Beat eggs and sugar in small bowl with electric mixer until thick and creamy, pour into heatproof bowl or top of double saucepan, stir over simmering water until mixture thickens slightly, cool to room temperature. Stir in chocolate, fold in cream. Pour into lamington pan, cover, freeze until almost set.

Egg yolks: Melt chocolate and butter over hot water, stir in icing sugar, brandy, reserved cream and hazelnuts, refrigerate several hours. Roll teaspoonfuls of mixture into balls, refrigerate before using.

1 **Chocolate shells:** Melt compound chocolate over hot water; spread a thin even layer of chocolate inside each half of egg moulds, refrigerate 5 minutes or until chocolate is set. Spread evenly with another thin layer of chocolate; keep chocolate as smooth as possible around the edge of mould, refrigerate until chocolate is set. Chocolate will shrink slightly from edges of moulds when ready, remove shells from each mould. Repeat with moulds to make 8 halves.

2 Fill 4 halves of eggs with partly set "egg white" ice-cream, place an "egg yolk" in centre of each half, stand on tray covered with folded tea towels, topped with a piece of waxed paper: this helps balance the eggs. Freeze 1 hour or until set. Beat remaining ice-cream with spoon until smooth, almost fill remaining 4 halves of eggs.

3 Spread a little melted chocolate around rim of each egg. Position evenly on towel-covered tray.

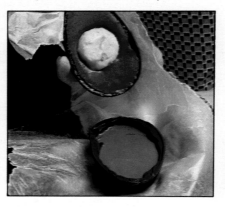

4 Place frozen egg halves on top, freeze overnight or until set. Makes 4.

HOME-MADE EASTER EGGS

Several brands and types of Easter egg moulds are available from chain and hardware stores. They are made from plastic; there is no need to grease or treat the egg moulds. It is

Home-made Easter Eggs

important to use the chocolate specified; eggs made from this will retain their gloss and shape at room temperature. The 375g chocolate will make 2 large and 2 small eggs.

**375g dark compound cooking
   chocolate, chopped
Easter egg moulds
ribbons and decorations**

Place chocolate in top of double saucepan or heatproof bowl, melt over simmering water. Spread a thin layer of chocolate inside mould, right up to the edge, refrigerate about 5 minutes or until chocolate is set. Then spread evenly with another layer of chocolate; keep chocolate as smooth as possible on edge of mould.

Refrigerate further 5 or 10 minutes

until chocolate has set; chocolate will shrink away slightly from side of mould when it is ready. Gently ease mould away from edge of chocolate; egg shape will fall easily from the mould. Join halves with a little more chocolate spread around edges. Decorate eggs with ribbon and flowers; use tiny dabs of chocolate to stick the decorations to the eggs.

PARTY
◆Cakes & Treats◆

*A selection of taste sensations for children's
parties; sweet and savoury treats and some
terrific novelty cakes will combine to make their
special day a memorable success.*

Chairs: Freedom Furniture; plates: Dansab; cups, jug & house: Fitz & Floyd

Clockwise from top: Corn and Cheese Muffins; Carrot Cars; Monster Dip

103

PARTY
SAVOURY TREATS

MONSTER DIP

Dip can be prepared the day before required and corn chips added just before the party. This recipe is not suitable to freeze.

250g packet cream cheese
300g carton sour cream
½ × 35g packet French onion soup mix
130g can corn kernels, drained
200g packet corn chips
2 black olives

Beat soft cream cheese in small bowl with electric mixer until smooth, beat in sour cream and soup mix, stir in corn. Place mixture onto centre of large plate, shape into a mound. Push corn chips into the dip, use olives for eyes of monster.
Serves 8.

CARROT CARS

Make these on day of serving, cover, keep refrigerated. This recipe is not suitable to freeze.

6 carrots, peeled
250g packet cream cheese
¼ cup finely chopped sultanas
¼ cup finely chopped walnuts
1 teaspoon grated lemon rind
currants
slivered almonds

Slice one of the carrots thinly to represent wheels. Cut remaining carrots in half lengthways, cut into pieces about 5cm long to represent the bodies.

Beat soft cream cheese in small bowl with electric mixer until smooth. Reserve about 2 tablespoons cheese. Stir sultanas, walnuts and lemon rind into bowl of cream cheese. Use reserved cream cheese to attach wheels to bodies of cars. Spread cheese mixture onto each car. Use the currants for headlights and slivered almonds for windows. Refrigerate, covered, until ready to serve.
Makes 10.

CORN AND CHEESE MUFFINS

These muffins are best made and eaten on the same day; serve buttered. Cooked muffins can be frozen for up to a month. This recipe is not suitable to microwave.

1 onion, finely chopped
4 bacon rashers, finely chopped
1½ cups self-raising flour
30g butter
1 cup grated tasty cheese
300g can creamed corn
⅓ cup milk
1 egg, lightly beaten

Cook onion and bacon in frying pan until onion is soft; drain on absorbent paper, cool.

Sift flour into large bowl, rub in butter. Stir in half the cheese and all the bacon mixture. Make well in centre of ingredients, stir in corn, milk and egg, mix only until ingredients are combined. Place tablespoons of mixture into greased muffin pans, sprinkle with remaining cheese. Bake in moderately hot oven for about 20 minutes; turn onto wire rack to cool.
Makes 24.

SAUSAGE POTS

Try to select even-shaped potatoes. Prepare sausage pots up to stage of cooking the day before required. This recipe is not suitable to freeze.

4 large potatoes
oil
8 processed cheese slices
FILLING
30g butter
4 thick sausages
15g butter, extra
4 green shallots, chopped
1 large tomato, peeled, chopped
¼ cup tomato sauce

Brush potatoes with oil, place into a baking dish, bake in moderate oven for about 1 hour or until tender.

Cut potatoes in half, scoop out a little potato from the centre of each half. Spoon filling into each potato half, top with a cheese slice. Bake in moderate oven for about 20 minutes or until heated through (or microwave on HIGH for about 5 minutes).
Filling: Heat butter in frying pan, add sausages, fry on all sides until golden brown and cooked through, drain on absorbent paper, slice sausages. Heat extra butter in frying pan, add shallots, tomato and tomato sauce, cover, bring to the boil, reduce heat, simmer uncovered for 5 minutes or until tomato is tender. Stir in sausages.
Makes 8.

Clockwise from top: Frankfurt Boats; Mini Pizza Torpedoes; Sausage Pots

Serving plates: Hale Imports 'Pillivuyt'; place mat & plates: Roussel Trading; mugs & jug: Fitz & Floyd

PARTY

FRANKFURT BOATS

Boats can be prepared up to the stage of cooking and kept covered in refrigerator for up to 12 hours. This recipe is not suitable to freeze or microwave.

20 slices white bread
2 tablespoons tomato sauce
1 teaspoon Worcestershire sauce
1 tablespoon chutney
20 cocktail frankfurts
30g butter, melted
2 tomatoes, sliced

Remove crusts from bread, roll bread with rolling pin to flatten. Spread each slice with combined sauces and chutney, top with frankfurts. Roll up, secure with toothpick. Brush each boat with butter, place boats on oven tray. Bake in moderately hot oven for about 10 minutes or until golden brown. Secure tomato slices to boats with toothpicks for sails.

Makes 20.

MINI PIZZA TORPEDOES

Torpedoes can be frozen for up to 2 months. Use your favourite pizza toppings. This recipe is not suitable to microwave.

6 finger bread rolls
3 tablespoons tomato paste,
  approximately
1 cup finely grated tasty cheese
10 slices salami, finely chopped
3 green shallots, chopped
5 black olives, pitted, chopped

Cut each bread roll in half lengthways, hollow out the centre. Spread each half with tomato paste, fill cavity with cheese, sprinkle with salami, shallots and olives. Bake in a moderate oven for about 10 minutes or until the cheese is melted.

Makes 12.

NAME PLACE CRACKERS

Let your imagination loose with these faces, perhaps the guest of honour could decorate them for friends.

Mixture for topping can be made the day before and kept in refrigerator. Allow to return to room temperature before spreading over crackers. Decorate crackers just before the party, so they don't soften. This recipe is not suitable to freeze or microwave.

4 hard-boiled eggs
15g soft butter
2 teaspoons mayonnaise
¼ teaspoon curry powder
8 large water crackers
2 tablespoons soft cream cheese

Push eggs through a fine sieve, com-

Clockwise from top: Sausage Pineapple Slice; Pretty Pinwheel Salad; Name Place Crackers

Pig: Fitz & Floyd; round plate: Dansab; rectangular plate: 'Pillivuyt' Hale Imports

bine with butter, mayonnaise and curry powder. Spread mixture evenly onto crackers. Cut various shapes out of vegetables, decorate as desired. Beat cream cheese until smooth, place into piping bag fitted with plain tube (or, make a paper bag, see page 120). Pipe children's names on crackers.

Makes 8.

SAUSAGE PINEAPPLE SLICE

Slice can be made the day before required, if preferred. Reheat in moderate oven for about 15 minutes. It can be frozen for up to 3 months. This recipe is not suitable to microwave.

2 ready-rolled puff pastry sheets
milk
FILLING
450g can crushed pineapple, drained
750g sausage mince
⅓ cup tomato sauce
4 green shallots, chopped
Cut one pastry sheet into two rectangles, 11cm × 25cm and 14cm × 25cm. Place the small rectangle onto a greased Swiss roll pan. Top with half the sausage filling, leaving a 2cm border around the edges, glaze with a little milk. Fold large rectangle in half lengthways, cut folded side at 1cm intervals, cutting to within 1cm of the opposite edge. Unfold pastry, place over filling, press edges together, brush with a little more milk. Repeat with remaining pastry and filling.

Bake in hot oven 10 minutes, reduce heat to moderate, bake further 45 minutes or until lightly browned. Drain fat from pan halfway through cooking time. Stand 5 minutes before serving.
Filling: Press out as much syrup from pineapple as possible. Combine pineapple with mince, tomato sauce and shallots, mix well.

Makes 2.

PRETTY PINWHEEL SALAD

Salad can be made a few hours ahead and stored covered in refrigerator.

2 butter lettuce
250g packet processed cheddar
    cheese
4 tomatoes, sliced
1 cucumber
450g can sliced pineapple, drained
2 oranges
DRESSING
¼ cup mayonnaise
2 tablespoons sweetened
    condensed milk
1 tablespoon white vinegar
Wash and dry lettuce, place on serving plate. Cut cheese into wedges, place on lettuce, top with tomatoes. Peel cu-

Left: Magic Cubes; right: Chocolate Mice

cumber, run a fork down the cucumber, slice thinly, place over tomatoes; top with halved pineapple. Segment oranges, removing all white pith, place over pineapple. Top with dressing just before serving.
Dressing: Combine all ingredients in small bowl.

Serves 8.

SWEET TREATS

MAGIC CUBES

Cake is easier to handle if it is a day old. The cubes can be made a day before required and stored uncovered in refrigerator. This recipe is not suitable to freeze or microwave.

2 packets buttercake or sponge mix
1 quantity chocolate Vienna cream
    (see page 112)
750g coloured sweets

Make cakes as directed on packets, spread evenly into well-greased 23cm square slab pan. Bake in moderate oven for about 45 minutes. Turn onto wire rack to cool. Trim sides and top of cake to make flat. Cut cake into 16 cubes using depth of cake as a guide. Freeze cubes for about an hour before icing. Spread cubes with Vienna cream, place sweets in position as shown in picture.

The easiest way to handle the cubes is to hold each piece of cake with thumb and middle finger, top and bottom. Spread 4 sides with cream, place sweets in position, then place cube on bench, sweets side down (they will not move out of position), spread one exposed side with cream and decorate with sweets. Stand with the other exposed end facing up and finish top of cube.

Makes 16.

CHOCOLATE UMBRELLAS

Umbrellas can be made up to a week before required (put in doiley cones on day of serving); keep refrigerated. This recipe is not suitable to freeze or microwave. A compound cooking chocolate can be used instead of the Copha and drinking chocolate; you will need about 250g chocolate.

90g Copha
1 cup drinking chocolate
60g (½ cup) unsalted roasted
   peanuts, chopped
7 plastic straws
paper doilies, about 18cm diameter
ribbon

To make paper cones to hold the chocolate, cut 7 × 12cm squares of greaseproof or baking paper (see page 120 on how to make paper bags). Fill a deep dish with uncooked rice and place paper cones point-side down into the rice to support the cones in an upright position.

Melt Copha in saucepan over low heat, stir in sifted drinking chocolate and peanuts. Fill cones with slightly cooled chocolate mixture. Refrigerate 5 minutes or until chocolate is just beginning to set. Cut straws in half; place a straw in each cone for the handle, refrigerate until set. Peel away paper.

Cut doilies in half, make into cones the same shape as the umbrellas. Insert chocolate umbrellas into fancy cones. Tie ribbon around each handle.
Makes 14.

Chocolate Umbrellas

CHOCOLATE MICE

The coconut is not affected by the marshmallow in this recipe, it can be used again. This recipe is not suitable to freeze or microwave.

¾ cup water
1 tablespoon gelatine
1 cup sugar
1 teaspoon lemon juice
750g (8 cups) coconut,
   approximately
125g Copha
1⅓ cups drinking chocolate
pipe cleaners
flaked almonds
silver cachous

Place water into saucepan, sprinkle gelatine over water, add sugar. Stir constantly over heat, without boiling, until sugar is dissolved. Boil uncovered, without stirring, for 5 minutes; cool to lukewarm. Pour mixture into small bowl of electric mixer, add lemon juice. Beat on high for 5 to 10 minutes or until marshmallow is thick and creamy, but still pourable.

Merry Mice

Spread coconut evenly into large baking dish. Press a large egg on its side halfway down into coconut. Do this at 2cm intervals, make 12 hollows.

Spoon marshmallow into hollows in coconut bringing it right to the top of the hollow. Leave for about 15 minutes or until set. Sprinkle coconut over tops of marshmallows. Gently lift marshmallows out of coconut, place on wire rack with a tray underneath.

Cut pipe cleaners in half, curl slightly, insert into marshmallows for tails. Melt Copha over low heat, stir in sifted drinking chocolate. Cool slightly before pouring over marshmallows, refrigerate 5 minutes or until set, spoon another layer of chocolate over the first layer. Use flaked almonds for ears and cachous for eyes. Refrigerate until chocolate has set.

Makes 12.

MERRY MICE

Mice can be completed a day before required. This recipe is not suitable to freeze or microwave.

1 cup plain flour
1 tablespoon castor sugar

1 tablespoon cocoa
60g butter
1 egg yolk
1 teaspoon lemon juice
1 tablespoon water, approximately
1 quantity Vienna cream (see page 112)
2 tablespoons cocoa, extra
2 teaspoons milk
slivered almonds
silver cachous
egg noodles
chocolate sprinkles
musk stick

Sift flour, sugar and cocoa into bowl, rub in butter. Add egg yolk and lemon juice, then enough water to make ingredients just cling together. (Pastry can also be made in a food processor.) Press pastry into a ball, cover, refrigerate 15 minutes.

Roll out pastry on lightly floured board. Cut out 5cm rounds with fluted cutter, place rounds in shallow patty pans, prick well all over with a fork. Bake in moderately hot oven for about 10 minutes or until pastry cases are lightly browned; cool in pans.

Fill piping bag fitted with small star tube with white Vienna cream. Pipe

ring of cream around edge of each pastry case. Stir extra sifted cocoa and milk into remaining Vienna cream. Place chocolate mixture into piping bag which has been fitted with plain 1cm tube. Pipe chocolate cream in centre. Use almonds for ears, cachous for eyes and nose, break off small pieces of egg noodles for whiskers. Sprinkle chocolate sprinkles over white cream. Use slices of musk stick for flowers.

Makes about 18.

LAMINGTON PRAMS

Cake is best made on the day before required, to prevent cake crumbling while being iced. This recipe is not suitable to freeze or microwave.

2 packets buttercake or sponge mix
16 chocolate bears
1 quantity of Vienna cream (see page 112)
CHOCOLATE ICING
2 cups icing sugar
2 tablespoons cocoa
½ cup milk
2 cups coconut, approximately

Make cakes as directed on packets,

place into well-greased 23cm square slab pan. Bake in moderate oven for about 45 minutes. Turn onto wire rack to cool.

Trim sides and top of cake to make flat. Cut cake into 16 squares, place in freezer while preparing icing.

Cut a slice — not quite through — to represent the hood of the pram. Spread inside of hood with Vienna cream. Push bear into cake against hood. Pipe Vienna cream around edge as shown. Use a pipe cleaner for pram handle. Use sweets for wheels and decorations.

Chocolate Icing: Sift icing sugar and cocoa into heatproof bowl, stir in milk gradually, stir until smooth. Stir icing constantly over simmering water until icing is thin and spreadable. Cover cakes with icing, toss cakes in coconut, stand on wire rack until icing is set. Refrigerate cakes for 2 hours.

Makes 16.

MERINGUE CLOWNS

This recipe is not suitable to freeze or microwave.

1 egg white
¾ cup castor sugar
2 teaspoons cornflour
1 teaspoon white vinegar
1 teaspoon vanilla essence
2 tablespoons boiling water
½ cup shredded coconut
yellow food colouring
1 cup icing sugar
1 tablespoon milk, approximately
hundreds and thousands
6 round ice-cream cones
assorted sweets

Combine egg white, sugar, cornflour, vinegar, essence and boiling water in small bowl of electric mixer, beat on high speed for about 10 minutes or until sugar is dissolved. Place mixture into piping bag fitted with a plain tube. Pipe six rounds onto a foil-covered oven tray. Bake in very slow oven for about 1 hour, or until dry to touch, cool in oven with door ajar.

Colour coconut by adding 1 teaspoon water to about ¼ teaspoon food colouring, add to coconut, mix well.

Sift the icing sugar into small heatproof bowl, add enough milk to give a fairly stiff paste, stir mixture over simmering water until icing is spreadable. Drizzle icing over cones, sprinkle with hundreds and thousands and stand on wire rack until icing is set. Use a little icing to secure sweets to meringue for eyes, mouth and nose. Sprinkle meringues with coconut for hair, place cones on top.

Makes 6.

TOP: Lamington Prams. ABOVE: Meringue Clowns

PARTY CAKES

RAINBOW

Rainbow cake can be made a day before required. Store in refrigerator if weather is hot. This recipe is not suitable to freeze or microwave.

2 packets buttercake or sponge mix
1½ quantities of Vienna cream
   (see below)
40cm round covered board
coconut
red, yellow, green, blue and violet
   food colouring
coloured sweets
silver cachous
chocolate money

Grease a deep 30cm round cake pan. Make cakes as directed on packets; pour into prepared pan, bake in moderate oven for about 45 minutes. Turn cake onto wire rack to cool.

Cut cake into rainbow shape as shown, cut away top of cake on an angle about halfway down the rainbow to give a sloping effect. Place cake on board. Cover sides of cake with Vienna cream, press coconut onto cream. Reserve ½ cup cream for the pot of gold. Divide remaining cream into 5 equal parts, colour each part with the colours above.

Mark lines on cake with point of a knife or skewer to use as a guide, spread in colours as shown, outline colours with sweets and cachous. Cut a pot shape from remaining cake, cover with cream, press coconut around sides, fill with money.

VIENNA CREAM

This recipe is not suitable to freeze.

125g butter
1½ cups icing sugar
2 tablespoons milk

Have butter at room temperature, cream butter in small bowl with electric mixer until as white as possible and light and fluffy, gradually beat in half the sifted icing sugar, all the milk, then the remaining icing sugar. Flavour and colour as desired.

Chocolate variation: Sift in ⅓ cup cocoa with the icing sugar.

FLUFFY FROSTING

This recipe is not suitable to freeze or microwave.

1 cup sugar
⅓ cup water
2 egg whites

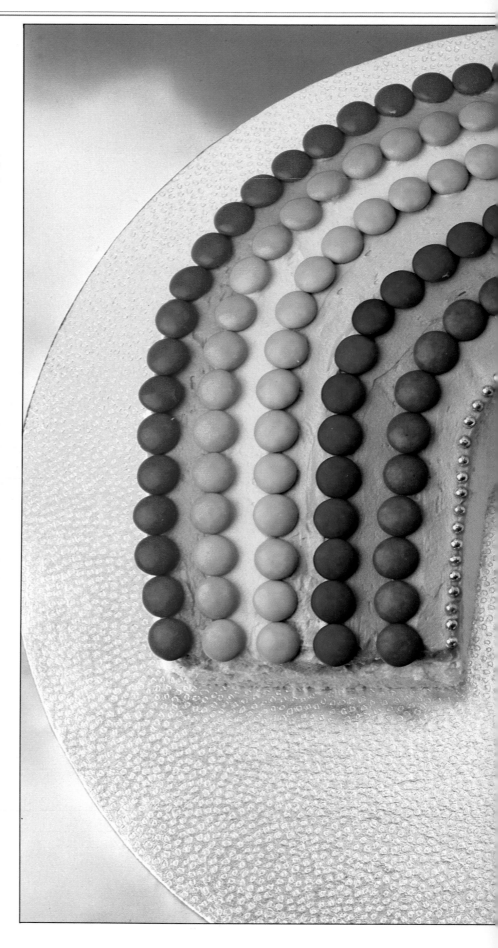

Rainbow Cake

Combine sugar and water in a small saucepan and stir constantly over heat, without boiling, until sugar is dissolved. Boil rapidly uncovered, without stirring, for 3 to 5 minutes. If a candy thermometer is available, the syrup should reach 114°C (240°F), otherwise test it by dropping 1 teaspoon of the sugar syrup into a cup of cold water. The syrup should form a ball of soft, sticky toffee when rolled gently between your fingers.

If testing syrup in water, remove pan from heat when syrup falls from spoon in a heavy drop; allow bubbles to subside, then test in cold water. The syrup should not change colour; if it does, it has been cooked for too long and you will have to throw out that batch and start again.

While syrup is boiling, beat egg whites in small bowl with electric mixer until stiff, keep beating (or whites will deflate) while syrup is reaching the correct temperature. When syrup is ready, allow bubbles to subside, pour in a very thin stream onto the egg whites while they are beating on a medium speed.

If syrup is added too quickly, frosting will not thicken. Continue beating and adding syrup until all syrup is used. Continue to beat until frosting will stand in stiff peaks (frosting should be only warm at this stage). Tint, if desired, by beating food colouring through in mixer or stirring through with spatula. Frosting also can be flavoured with ½ teaspoon of any essence of your choice.

For best results, frosting should be applied to a cake on the day it is to be served, while frosting is beautifully soft, with a marshmallow consistency. The cake can be frosted the day before; however, frosting will become slightly crisp because it has dried out a little and will lose its glossy appearance. Make sure to frost cake around the base near the board; this will form a seal and help keep the cake fresh.

LIGHTHOUSE

You will need a large serving plate for this recipe; we used a glass platter. Make on the day of serving. This recipe is not suitable to freeze or microwave.

1 packet buttercake mix
1 quantity fluffy frosting
   (see page 112)
licorice strands and allsorts
8 × 100g packets lime jelly
1kg rocky road
Make cake as directed on packet.

Lighthouse Cake

Spread into well-greased 25cm × 30cm Swiss roll pan. Bake in a moderate oven for about 25 minutes. Turn onto wire rack to cool. Cut nine circles from the cake; you will need 3 × 8cm, 2 × 7½cm, 2 × 6½cm, 1 × 4cm and 1 × 3cm circles. Join circles with a little frosting (starting with the largest) on a saucer to form the lighthouse.

Spread lighthouse with frosting. Use licorice and allsorts for windows and lights. Make jelly according to directions on packets, pour into bowls; refrigerate until set.

Place lighthouse onto serving plate, use rocky road for rocks around the base of the lighthouse and chopped jelly for water.

AUSSIE RULES CAKE

This cake is for a large party. This recipe is not suitable to freeze or microwave.

5 packets buttercake or sponge mix
70cm square board
4 quantities Vienna cream
(see page 112)
brown and green food colouring
1 cup coconut
½ cup chocolate sprinkles
assorted sweets

Make cakes individually as directed on packets. Place the cake mixtures into four well-greased 23cm square slab pans. Divide the remaining cake mixture between two well-greased 8cm × 26cm bar pans. Bake cakes in moderate oven for about 35 minutes. Turn onto wire racks to cool.

Colour half the Vienna cream brown, colour two-thirds of the remaining cream green, leave remaining third white.

Place all four square cakes side by side on board for the base of the field. Trim tops of cakes to make them level. Cut top from bar cakes to make them level. Cut bar cakes in half diagonally (from corner to opposite corner) for the grandstands. Place bar cakes on each side of the field, trim to fit.

Mark the oval boundary with the tip of a sharp knife or skewer, spread evenly with the green cream, cover with coconut. Spread the rest of the cake evenly with brown cream, sprinkle border with chocolate sprinkles, as shown. Place white cream in piping bag (or paper bag see page 120) fitted with plain tube, pipe markings, as shown. Decorate with sweets. We used eight chocolate cigarettes for the goal posts, licorice allsort triangles on toothpicks for flags and a brown jelly bean for the ball.

Aussie Rules Cake

Clarence Crocodile Cake

PARTY

CLARENCE CROCODILE

Clarence can be made a day before required. Keep refrigerated if weather is hot. This recipe is not suitable to freeze or microwave.

2 packets buttercake or sponge mix
30cm × 50cm covered board
2 quantities Vienna cream
  (see page 112)
caramel, yellow and green food
  colouring
licorice
licorice allsorts

Make cakes as directed on packets. Divide between 2 well-greased 23cm square cake pans. Bake in moderate oven for about 30 minutes. Turn onto wire racks to cool.

Place cakes side by side on board. Spread top and sides of cake with half the Vienna cream. Tint a quarter of a cup of the cream with caramel colouring, pipe outline of crocodile. Tint a third of remaining cream with yellow colouring, spread evenly as shown. Tint remaining cream with green colouring. Pipe and spread cream as shown. Use licorice for claws and eyes and the white of allsorts for the teeth.

MAKING A PAPER PIPING BAG

Cut a 30cm square of greaseproof paper in half diagonally to give two triangles. Wrap the paper around to form a cone. Hold the apex towards you, bring right point to apex. Wrap left point anti-clockwise to meet these points. Hold the cone with both hands, thumbs inside, and slide the two outside points in opposite directions to draw cone tip into a tight sharp point.

Sticky-tape the outside seam of the cone near the top to hold it together. Cut the tip of the cone into a V shape.

SPRING BONNET

Bonnet can be made a day ahead. Store in refrigerator if the weather is hot. This recipe is not suitable to freeze or microwave.

2 packets buttercake or sponge mix
2 quantities Vienna cream
  (see page 112)
lemon food colouring
40cm round covered board
silver cachous
sugared violets and mint leaves
  (see below)
ribbon

Make cakes as directed on packets, pour mixture into a well-greased 4 cup capacity pudding steamer to three-quarters full. Bake (without lid) in moderate oven for about 1 hour. Turn onto a wire rack to cool.

Pour remaining mixture into well-greased deep 30cm round cake pan. Bake in moderate oven for about 45 minutes. Turn onto wire rack to cool.

Assemble cakes on board to form bonnet shape. Tint Vienna cream with lemon (this colouring tends to darken on standing) colouring. Spread cakes with cream; decorate with cachous, violets, mint leaves and ribbon.

SUGARED MINT LEAVES AND VIOLETS

Sugared leaves and violets can be stored in an airtight container for up to 2 months.

1 cup castor sugar
purple and green food colouring
1 egg white
fresh mint leaves
fresh violets

1 Divide sugar in half. Place into separate plastic bags. Add a few drops of purple food colouring to one bag; rub colouring through sugar by rubbing outside of plastic bag with hand. Add a few drops of green food colouring to remaining sugar; repeat process to colour sugar.

2 Use small artists' paintbrush to brush egg white evenly, but sparingly over both sides of mint leaves and violets. Make sure to brush egg white in between petals.

3 Sprinkle violets with purple sugar and mint leaves with green sugar; shake off excess sugar. Stand on wire rack in a warm, dry place until violets and leaves are dry.

TERRY TARANTULA

The cake can be completed up to 2 days ahead of the party; refrigerate if weather is hot. This recipe is not suitable to freeze or microwave.

1½ packets buttercake or
  sponge mix
40cm round covered board
32 pipe cleaners
sweets
coconut
1 quantity Vienna cream
  (see page 112)

Make cake as directed on packet. Pour mixture into large well-greased aluminium pudding steamer, 3¾ litre (15-cup fluid capacity), bake (without lid) in moderately slow oven for about 1¼ hours, turn onto wire rack to cool.

When cake is cold, trim top so cake will sit flat when inverted onto board. Spread cake with Vienna cream, decorate with sweets. We used four pipe cleaners for each leg, two twisted together, joined at the "bend" with another two twisted together. Surround Terry with green coconut to represent grass, if desired.

Terry Tarantula Cake

ABOVE: 'Shemozzle', the Koala Cake
RIGHT: Sweet Heart Cake

'SHEMOZZLE', THE KOALA

This recipe is not suitable to freeze or microwave. The design of this cake was by Murray Van Hooroo Studio, North Sydney, NSW.

2 packets buttercake or sponge mix
50cm round covered board
1½ quantities Vienna cream (see page 112)
brown, pink and yellow food colouring
licorice
chocolate sprinkles
soft jubes
2 white marshmallows
2 chocolate-coated biscuits

Make cakes as directed on packets, divide mixture between 2 well-greased deep 18cm round cake pans and a well-greased deep 20cm round cake pan. Bake in moderate oven for 45 minutes. Turn onto wire racks to cool.

Trim the 2 small cakes, as shown, to represent "ears". Place cakes onto the prepared board, using the large cake for the face.

Tint quarter of the Vienna cream with brown food colouring, quarter with pink and remaining with yellow colouring. Spread sides of cake with brown cream. Spread bottom half of the face with pink cream, then top half of face and ears with yellow cream.

Outline face, ears and mouth with licorice. Sprinkle insides of ears with chocolate sprinkles. Use jubes for inside of mouth, marshmallows and licorice for eyes. Join biscuits together with a little cream, use for nose.

SWEET HEART

This cake would be delightful for a teenager, grandmother or for Mother's Day. It can be prepared a day before required. This recipe is not suitable to freeze or microwave.

1 packet buttercake or sponge mix
30cm round covered board
4 silver doilies
1 quantity fluffy frosting
   (see page 112)
pink food colouring
artificial flowers and leaves
pink candles
butterfly

Make cake as directed on packet. Pour mixture into a well-greased 25cm heart-shaped cake pan. Bake in moderate oven for about 40 minutes. Turn cake onto wire rack to cool.

   Place cake on board covered with doilies. Tint frosting with colouring, spread over cake. Arrange flowers, leaves, candles and butterfly as shown.

GLOSSARY

ALMONDS: use commercially ground almonds when recipe specifies.

ARROWROOT: a thickening ingredient; cornflour can be substituted.

BEETROOT: regular round beet.

BICARBONATE OF SODA: baking soda.

BREADCRUMBS: *Stale:* use 1 or 2 day old white or wholemeal bread made into crumbs by grating, blending or processing. *Packaged:* use commercially packaged breadcrumbs.

BUTTER: we use salted butter unless otherwise specified; a good quality cooking margarine can be used if preferred.

BUTTERMILK: the liquid left from separated cream, slightly sour in taste; use skim milk if unavailable.

CHESTNUT PUREE: is an unsweetened puree of chestnuts. Do not confuse with the sweetened flavoured chestnut spread.

CHICKEN: numbers indicate the weight, for example: No.13 chicken weighs 1.3kg. This applies to all poultry.

CHILLI POWDER: the Asian variety of the powder is the hottest and is made from ground dried chillies; it can be used as a chilli substitute for fresh chillies in the proportion of ½ teaspoon ground chilli powder to 1 medium chopped chilli.

CHILLI SAUCE: we used a hot Chinese variety. It consists of chillies, salt and vinegar. We used it sparingly so that you can easily increase amounts in recipes to suit your taste.

CHOCOLATE: *Choc-bits* and *Milk-bits:* are small buds of compound chocolate. *Compound:* a cooking chocolate with additives which does not need tempering to maintain a shape at room temperature. *Dark:* we used a good quality cooking chocolate. *Milk:* we used a light chocolate bar. *White:* we used a white chocolate bar.

COPHA: solid white shortening based on coconut oil; no known substitute.

CORNFLOUR: cornstarch.

CREAM: we have specified thickened (whipping) cream when necessary in recipes; cream is simply a light pouring cream, also known as half 'n' half. *Sour:* a thick commercially cultured soured cream. *Light sour:* a less dense commercially cultured soured cream.

CUSTARD POWDER: pudding mix.

ESSENCE: extract.

FRESH GINGER: ginger root.

FRESH HERBS: we have specified when to use fresh or dried herbs, or given alternative measurements when possible. Usually we used dried (not ground) herbs in the proportion of 1:4 for fresh herbs, eg. 1 teaspoon dried herbs instead of 4 teaspoons (1 tablespoon) chopped fresh herbs.

GOLDEN SYRUP: maple/pancake syrup, honey can be substituted.

GREEN SHALLOTS: spring onions or scallions.

GRILL, GRILLER: broil/broiler.

GROUND ALMONDS/HAZELNUTS: we used pre-packaged ground nuts in our recipes unless otherwise specified.

GROUND RICE: rice flour can be substituted.

HUNDREDS AND THOUSANDS: nonpareils.

LIQUID GLUCOSE (glucose syrup): made from wheat starch; available at health food stores and supermarkets.

MIXED FRUIT: a combination of sultanas, raisins, currants, mixed peel and cherries.

MIXED PEEL: a mixture of chopped crystallised citrus peel.

MIXED SPICE: a finely ground combination of spices which include caraway, allspice, coriander, cumin, nutmeg, ginger and cinnamon; almost always used in sweet recipes. Do not confuse mixed spice with allspice.

MUESLI: crunchy granola.

OIL: we used a light polyunsaturated salad oil unless otherwise specified.

PEPPERS: capsicums or bell peppers.

PIMENTOS: allspice.

PIMIENTOS: canned or bottles peppers.

PLAIN FLOUR: all-purpose flour.

PUNNET: basket usually holding about 250g fruit.

RICE BUBBLES: rice crispies.

RICE FLOUR: ground rice can be substituted.

SELF-RAISING FLOUR: substitute plain (all-purpose) flour and baking powder in the proportion of ¾ metric cup plain flour to 2 level metric teaspoons baking powder, sift together several times before using. If using an 8oz measuring cup use 1 cup plain flour to 2 teaspoons baking powder.

STOCK CUBE: equivalent to 1 teaspoon powdered bouillon.

SUGAR, CASTOR: fine granulated table or berry sugar.

SUGAR: *Crystal:* use a coarse granulated table sugar. *Icing:* confectioners' or powdered sugar. We used icing sugar mixture (not pure) in the recipes in this book. *Raw:* natural light brown granulated sugar or "sugar in the raw" can be used.

SULTANAS: seedless white raisins.

SWEET BISCUITS: any plain sweet biscuit (or cookies) can be used.

TASTY CHEESE: use a hard good-tasting cheddar cheese.

VEGETABLES: we used all medium-sized vegetables in this book unless otherwise specified.

WINE: we used good quality red and white wines.

YEAST: allow 3 teaspoons (7g) dried granulated yeast to each 15g compressed yeast.

ZUCCHINI: courgette.

INDEX